Knitted Lace Doilies

Knitted Lace Doilies

First published by The Thorn Press in 1986

Facsimile Edition published in 2014
ISBN 978-0-906374-54-2

THE THORN PRESS
WWW.THETHORNPRESS.COM

TESSA LORANT

KNITTED LACE DOILIES

Chinese Lantern Table Centre

THE THORN PRESS

KNITTING PUBLICATONS
BY
TESSA LORANT

THE BATSFORD BOOK OF HAND AND MACHINE KNITTING
THE BATSFORD BOOK OF HAND AND MACHINE KNITTED LACES
YARNS FOR TEXTILE CRAFTS

THE HERITAGE OF KNITTING SERIES

TESSA LORANT'S COLLECTION OF KNITTED LACE EDGINGS
KNITTED QUILTS & FLOUNCES
KNITTED LACE COLLARS
KNITTED SHAWLS & WRAPS
THE SECRETS OF SUCCESSFUL IRISH CROCHET LACE
KNITTED LACE DOILIES

THE PROFITABLE KNITTING SERIES
EARNING AND SAVING WITH A KNITTING MACHINE
CHOOSING AND BUYING A KNITTING MACHINE
YARNS FOR THE KNITTER
THE GOOD YARN GUIDE

ACKNOWLEDGMENTS

This book includes some enchanting new doilies designed by Mary Medlar. I would like to thank Mary for sharing her doily designs as well as her personal methods for working KNITTED CHAINS and LOOPED KNITTED PICOTS with other knitters. My thanks to Mary, too, for carefully checking the typeset versions of her patterns.

Thanks are also due to the late Ayliffe Hervey. As so often, her perfect knitting displays my own designs, as well as the adapted and traditional knitting patterns used in this book, beautifully. I would also like to express my appreciation to Ayliffe for patiently checking my new design ideas as well as my new knitting methods and techniques.

THE HERITAGE OF KNITTING SERIES
Facsimile editions are in preparation by The Thorn Press.
Please check for available titles on Amazon or in good bookshops.

THE HERITAGE OF KNITTING SERIES

FACSIMILE EDITIONS IN PREPARATION: AVAILABLE THROUGH 2014

TESSA LORANT

WWW.TESSALORANTWARBURG.COM

TESSA LORANT'S COLLECTION OF KNITTED LACE EDGINGS
PAPERBACK: ISBN 978-0-906374-50-4 (FEBRUAY 2014

KNITTED QUILTS & FLOUNCES
PAPERBACK: ISBN 978-0-906374-29-0 (2012)

KNITTED LACE DOILIES
PAPERBACK: ISBN 978-0-906374-54-2

KNITTED LACE COLLARS
PAPERBACK: ISBN 978-0-906374-51-1

KNITTED SHAWLS & WRAPS
PAPERBACK: ISBN 978-0-906374-52-8

THE SECRETS OF IRISH CROCHET LACE
PAPERBACK: ISBN 978-0-906374-53-5

ONTENTS

* means suitable for beginners to try.

ABBREVIATIONS

If a number follows an abbreviation, or a set of abbreviations in brackets, then the action is repeated that number of times:

K6 = knit 6 sts; PT2 = purl, wrapping yarn **twice** round (or over) the RHN;
O2 = wrap the yarn **twice** round (or over) the RHN; (P2, K3)2 = P2, K3, P2, K3.

If an asterisk (*) follows an abbreviation, or a set of abbreviations in brackets, the action is repeated to the last few stitches, or until the end of the row or round.

P* = purl the sts in the row or round;
K*, P3 = knit to the last 3 sts in the row or round, then P3;
(O, K2tog)*, K1 = knit (O, K2tog) to the last st in the row or round, then K1.

K*, + 1 = work the sts on each needle, then, before working the rest of the sts on the next needle, work the first stitch from the next needle onto the needle being used.

Knitting Abbreviations

K	=	knit.
P	=	purl.
K'	=	knit through the back of the loop.
P'	=	purl through the back of the loop.
c	=	cast on.
C	=	cast off.
O	=	one over (yarn round needle, yarn over needle), made by wrapping the yarn over the needle **without** working a stitch; i.e. O3 = wrap the yarn **three** times over the needle.
T	=	one throw, made by wrapping the yarn round the needle, **then** working a stitch, i.e. T2 = wrap the yarn **twice** round needle.
M	=	make one stitch by knitting into the yarn bar **between** two sts.
M'	=	make one stitch by knitting into the **back** of the yarn bar between two sts (so twisting the stitch).
Kbf	=	knit into the back and front of the same stitch.
U	=	turn, leaving sts 'in holding' on the needle used for knitting.
pnso, psso	=	pass next st over, pass slipped st or sts over.
pso	=	pass the **second** st on RHN over first, i.e. make a chain cast-off.
st, sts	=	stitch, stitches.
tog	=	together.
Sk	=	slip 1 st knitwise.
Sp	=	slip 1 st purlwise.
Ch	=	make a knitted chain. Ch4 means make a 4-st chain.
- n	=	knit to within 'n' sts of the end of each needle and transfer these sts to next needle. (Circular knitting).
+ n	=	after working the sts on each needle, knit on 'n' sts from the next needle, i.e. + 1 means knit on 1 st from the next needle.
LHS, LHN	=	left hand side, left hand needle.

RHS, RHN	=	right hand side, right hand needle.
Kntog	=	knit 'n' loops tog as though knitting 1 st, i.e. K2tog = K 2 sts tog.
SStog	=	Sk, Sk, knit these 2 sts off tog on RHN.
SKtog	=	Sk, K1, psso.
SK2tog	=	Sk, K2tog, psso.
SSKtog	=	Sk, Sk, K1, pass the **two** slipped stitches over.
SSK3tog	=	Sk, Sk, K3tog, pass the **two** slipped sts over.
Pntog	=	purl 'n' loops tog as though purling 1 st, i.e. P3tog = P 3 sts tog.
SPtog	=	Sp, P1, psso.
PStog	=	P1, slip back to LHN, pnso on LHN, return st to RHN.

Crochet Abbreviations

ch	=	chain.
dc	=	double crochet.
ss	=	slip stitch.

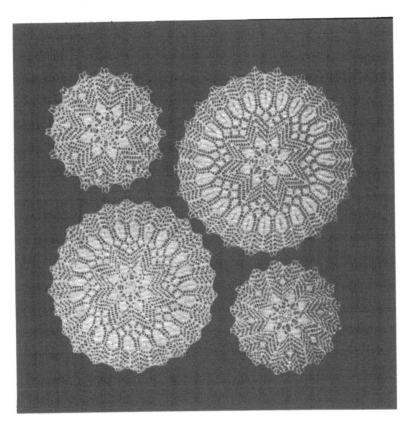

Two sets of SMALL and MEDIUM Acanthus Leaf Mats

The illustration shows the difference between merely good, and outstanding, dressing of the same knitted lace doilies. Really painstaking dressing displays the lace and outlines to their best advantage, and the doilies also grow larger.

This knitted-up version of the traditional **Dahlia Doily** design, with its sewn-on edging, shows the edging join rather clearly. The knitting was done on 2.75 mm (12s) needles and in Coats Mercer Crochet 10. The doily has a 34 cm (13.5 ins) diameter, and took roughly 30g of yarn. The traditional pattern is worked by making a purled ridge, followed by open knitting, followed by another ridge of reversed stocking stitch.

Traditional Dahlia Doily
Knitted by Queenie Hitchcock. Pattern as for **Dahlia Centre Pattern**, page 43, together with the finishing pattern, given on page 22.

6

Introduction

The word **doily** (variously spelt doiley, doyly, doyley and even, erroneously, d'oily, d'oiley, d'oyly or d'oilie) derives from the surnames of three men who originally furthered the fashion in such fabric pieces. According to the OED the first was a Mr **Doily**, known in 1712 for his flair in promoting materials 'at once cheap and genteel'. In 1727 another Mr **Doyly**, who was said to be keen on searching out unusual wear, introduced the doily as a fashion accessory, often in the form of a neckerchief. Finally, there was yet another Mr **Doyley**, whose linen-drapery in the Strand provided doilies for the public from 1750 - 1800.

The first use of the doily for the dining table was as a napkin, often used at dessert. In Victorian times the doily became very popular as an ornamental mat for cake plates. Doilies are still used in this way now, usually in the form of small lace mats, with their use extended to decorate tables and dressing tables, as well as cake stands and plates.

Lace doilies provide a simple way of adding that gracious touch to tables set for festive occasions - birthday teas, coffee parties, or even formal dinner parties. Lace doilies are easier to look after than lace tablecloths, and can readily be made in several different sizes in a matching pattern, so providing a matching set of place mats, glass mats and table centres. Apart from table decoration, doilies can be framed to make unusual and very attractive textile 'pictures'. They can also be embedded in plastic resin, to make coasters and heat-proof table mats, or they can be attractively displayed under a glass-topped table.

Pretty, mass-produced doilies of all kinds, even plastic ones, can readily be bought. But for the discerning homemaker these mass-produced articles are no substitute for handmade lace. And for the dedicated knitters, whether their skills are average or more advanced, knitting lace doilies provides a most delightful way of displaying that skill in the beautiful craft of lace knitting.

There are many patterns for crochet doilies, but **knitted** doily patterns are hard to find, both in modern and older publications. And, of the traditional patterns, most finish their doilies by using a suitable **knitted lace edging**. Unfortunately, this involves connecting the beginning and end of the lace edging, as well as connecting the edging to the central doily. Such joins can spoil the look of the carefully knitted lace, so part of the **Techniques** section gives methods of making the joins as unobtrusive as possible.

Traditional and Modern Designs

This book offers you a selection of traditional and modern knitted lace doily designs, for both the average and the expert knitter. Added to that are my own combinations of traditional lace edgings and doily centres, providing you with doily designs having the traditional look, in keeping with the **Heritage of Knitting** series. Furthermore, several of the doilies are knitted on two needles, a help for those knitters who do not like to knit in the round. It is, perhaps, because many modern knitters are reluctant to attempt circular knitting that doily patterns are not as common as they might be. This book also includes many designs knitted on four or more needles, in a range of very simple to quite sophisticated patterns. The simpler ones are starred (*).

Knitted Finishes

The more recent designs in circular doilies are generally finished with some sort of crochet edging, but many modern knitters do not like to crochet. Mary Medlam's knitted **Chain Cast-off,** and her **Knitted Picots,** which can readily replace the crochet used in most published patterns, will delight knitters who prefer not to crochet at all.

One of the important aspects of presenting knitted lace well is to finish the articles in keeping with the knitted pattern. My own **Frill Cast-off** is explained in the **Techniques** section. It is a simply knitted, yet ornamental, finish for those knitters who often find their cast-off row too tight. It is also eminently suitable for adding a knotted fringe as a means of finishing the doily. My **Loop Cast-on,** for circular knitting, may also be of interest to knitters who find it difficult to start circular work. There are one or two other, relatively unknown, techniques which are also explained, some of them published here for the first time. The crochet chain finish is explained for those who like this type of finish.

Making your own Doily Centre and Edging Combinations

Several of the designs can be interchanged to make new, individual combinations of your own, based on the patterns given here. **Any** sideways knitted, sufficiently curved, lace edging can be used to embellish or enlarge a doily centre with a plain outline. More edging patterns can be found in my **KNITTED LACE EDGINGS** (Thorn). Methods of making the inevitable join effectively invisible are given later, as already explained.

Yarns, Needles and Crochet Hooks

The yarns used to make the articles illustrated in this book are all crochet cottons from the Coats Mercer Crochet, Twilleys Forties, and South Maid ranges. These are the yarns most readily found in the High Street or the department store, but you can very easily substitute any yarn of your choice. The **Silver Gauge** (see inside back cover) rating or category will give you an indication of the range of yarns which will produce **similar** articles to the ones illustrated in this book, though of course the tension and 'feel' of the article may change considerably. Please also remember that knitters have their own, individual tension. The final size of the article will depend not only on the individual knitter's tension and the method of dressing, but also on the yarn and needle combination used. A range of useful needle sizes to work with is given in each pattern.

The most useful size of crochet hook, for those who prefer a crochet finish, or for those who like to latch up their knitted laces and do not have a latchet tool, is the 1.00 mm size.

The **weight** of each illustrated doily is given so that you can work out how much yarn you will need for the set of doilies you intend to make.

Dressing

The dressing of knitted laces, and its importance, has been discussed at length in my other books on knitted lace, particularly in **THE BATSFORD BOOK OF HAND AND MACHINE KNITTED LACES.** I will just emphasise again that all knitted lace fabric must be wetted, starched and then stretched into its correct shape for maximum effect. This last part is readily done by using polystyrene ceiling tiles as a base for pinning out. Cover the tiles with contrast-coloured, self-adhesive vinyl marked with appropriate circles or other shapes. The wetted lace can then be pinned out over the shapes on the vinyl.

Though dressing the **Festive Cake Frill** lace is not really different from dressing any of the other laces, it is useful to latch up the two sections, and to combine the cast-off and cast-on edges in each case, before wetting and starching the frill. Find a cylinder with the correct diameter for the 'cake' part of the frill, place this straight lace edging over the cylinder, stretching the lace out as required. Now place the whole set-up over a polystyrene base and spread out the frill. Pin to display the picots and lace points. Starch heavily so that the dried lace can stand by itself.

Washing Doilies

Since doilies are often used as table mats, they will need relatively frequent washing. You can, simply, soak the doilies in lukewarm water mixed with a suitable liquid cleansing agent, such as Woolite or Cool Force. Then gently squeeze the doilies, rinse thoroughly, and starch and dress the doilies as though they had just been knitted. There is no reason why you should not pin out a whole set of same-size, same-pattern doilies stacked on top of each other. On the contrary, this will ensure that they are all exactly the same size, though of course they will take longer to dry. Treat stains as you would for any other lace fabric.

An old-fashioned way of laundering lace is to wrap it round a glass bottle or other cylindrical glass shape, covering the lace with muslin to hold it in place. This ensures that the lace does not get snagged or otherwise damaged. Fill the glass container with sand to keep it steady and stand the whole contraption in a saucepan filled with cold water mixed with soapflakes or some other cleansing agent, covering the lace completely. Now gently heat the water. When it becomes dirty, pour it off and replace it with clean water. Continue to do this until the water is clear. Unwrap the lace, pat it dry between towels, then starch it and dress it as above.

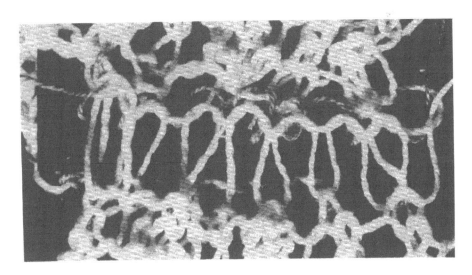

Grafting **In Pattern** (See page 10)

9

TECHNIQUES

The techniques given below have been included to help you get the most from the designs in this book. However, this is not a knitting manual. Please refer to my **BATSFORD BOOK OF HAND AND MACHINE KNITTED LACES,** or any other lace knitting manual, for general techniques of lace knitting.

Grafting

Grafting is a method of joining two pieces of knitting invisibly by threading a blunt-ended needle with the yarn used for the knitting, then combining two sets of open knitted loops with a row simulating the joining row between them.

There are two ways of joining open loops. One will imitate a knit, the other a purl, stitch. The best way to see how this is done is to make a small, stocking stitch swatch, using DK wool and 5 mm (6s) needles. Knit a few rows in the wool, then knit 1 row in a slippery, contrast yarn, then finish with a few rows wool. Unravel several contrast yarn stitches, thread your needle and, using the remaining stitches as a guide, graft the open loops together. Do this on both the plain and the purl sides.

Many knitters do not like to graft. They think it difficult to carry out, and think they will find it impossible to tension the grafted row in keeping with the rest of the work. However, grafting is one of the best ways of making invisible joins in knitted fabric and, once practised, is just as quick as any other form of seaming. Though some knitters eventually learn how to graft stocking stitch, and even garter stitch and ribs, pattern knitting, particularly lace knitting, is much harder to imitate. My method works for **any** knitted row using a continuous thread across the row (i.e. no pso, etc).

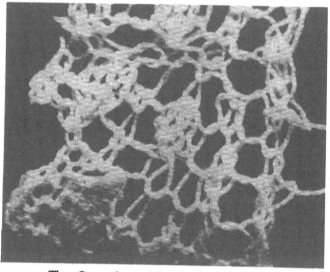

The Completed Graft **in Pattern**

Grafting in Pattern (Tessa Lorant)

Make yourself a small knitted swatch, using the yarn and needles you will use for the pattern. Make a **Knitted Cast-on** of, say, 30 stitches, knitting into the front of each stitch. Work 10 rows stocking stitch. Cast off and cut the yarn. Using the cast-on loops as a base, knit **the last pattern repeat row** of a particular pattern, in a fine yarn, using a contrast colour. Attach the beginning and end of this yarn to hold it firm. Reattach the knitting yarn and knit the **first** row of the pattern repeat. Knit the number of pattern repeats required, **leaving out the very last row.** Knit this in the same fine, contrast yarn as before. This is the row you will simulate by grafting.

Buy some self-adhesive vinyl, cut off pieces large enough to hold the two rows knitted in contrast yarn, and press the contrast-coloured loops onto the sticky side of the vinyl. This will hold the loops in place and stop them running, so you can pull out the knitting needle. Set these loops to face each other (as illustrated), and the knitting will be held ready for grafting. Thread your tapestry needle with the knitting yarn and simply follow the contrast threads with your needle, combining the two sections of the knitted fabric. Follow the **upper** loops of the first contrast row, and the **lower** loops of the second contrast row. Do not worry about the tension at this stage.

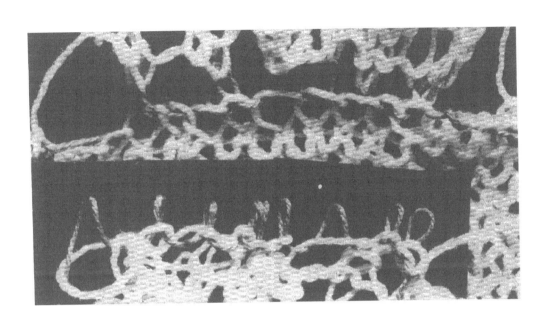

Tensioning the Grafted Row

When you have finished grafting the row, pull out the contrast yarns and remove the swatch. Replace your grafted section on the vinyl, turn it upside down for convenience, and adjust the tension of your grafted row as you would mend a snagged row - by pulling each loop to its correct size. Work from left to right so that you can place a left finger on each adjusted loop to hold it firm.

A pattern which has one row of plain or purl knitting is, of course, the easiest to use for grafting. Most edging patterns have at least **one** relatively simple pattern row. Adjust your pattern to make this the **last** row and use it for the grafting. You will have an invisible join which is relatively easy to make.

Practise with medium yarn and needles; once you have mastered the technique, you can use it to make an invisible join for most knitted lace edgings.

Semi grafting

You do not need two sets of open knitted loops. You can graft together open knitted loops and any other looped edge, such as a picot side selvedge, a **Knitted Cast-on**, or a **Frill Cast-off.**

Joining the Edging to the Lace Centre

Most traditional patterns tell you to sew the lace edging neatly to a plain, cast-off edge of the centre. This is never as good a method as knitting on, latching up, or grafting the lace edging to the centre.

Latching Up

Place the two pieces of knitting to be latched together side by side. Using a latchet tool, or a fine crochet hook, slip the hook through the first loop on the right hand side, then pull the first loop on the left hand side through this loop. Continue pulling through loops, alternatively from left to right to left, until the two pieces are joined. Pull a yarn end through the last loop and darn it in.

Picot Side Selvedge

The secret of grafting or latching up lies in having the correct selvedges for the purpose. Any knitted lace edging can have a picot selvedge on its straight (unserrated) side edge by working the first two stitches of one row: O, K2tog, and the last two stitches of the return row: K2. For **large** selvedge picots, which are best for latching up, replace O with O2, and drop the second loop on the return row.

Knitting the Edging in or on:

Do **not** cast off the last round of the central section, but leave the stitches on the set of needles you knitted with, or on a circular needle. Alternatively, use the **Frill Cast-off** (see below). Now, with the appropriate side of the doily facing you, use the first doily stitch as a base for casting on the edging. Knit back the foundation row, knitting the next stitch of the doily **together** with the last straight selvedge stitch. Alternatively, knit the last edging row in contrast yarn on your swatch, ready for an invisible grafting join when you have surrounded the doily centre. You will be knitting two rows for every central stitch you use, so make sure that half your edging **row** repeat is a factor of your last knitted round; for example, an eight row edging pattern needs to connect to a last round which is a multiple of four. Either choose an edging pattern which has the correct number of rows, or adjust the last knitted round by increasing or decreasing a few stitches symmetrically. Or, knit an easily adjusted reverse stocking stitch ridge (see page 22).

The last round may also be cast off, preferably using the **Frill Cast-off**. If you use a very much **larger** needle for this cast-off you will get quite large picots. These can be **latched up** to a picot border worked on the straight selvedge of a knitted lace edging. You will, again, have to ensure that your cast-off picots are a multiple of half your row repeats. You can also use smaller cast-off picots for **knitting on** a border, as above.

Alternatively, simply **graft** the straight, picot-edged side of a knitted lace edging to the last round of a central piece with an unserrated edge. Another solution is to make a small picot selvedge for the straight edge of the lace edging, cast off the centre using the **Frill Cast-off**, and graft or sew the two sets of picots together.

Any one of these joins will give you a completely **knitted** look for your finished piece. This provides you with the opportunity to use many different combinations of your favourite edging and centre patterns for making your own doily adaptations.

12

Useful Cast-ons

Open Loop Cast-on

Make a small stocking stitch, or garter stitch, swatch. Cast on, using the **Knitted Cast-on**, and work into the front of the stitches. Work a plain row, in a slippery, contrast yarn, on the cast-on loops, then work your pattern in the knitting yarn, starting with a plain foundation row. Pull out the contrast yarn and slip the open loops onto a needle, ready for grafting.

Knitted Cast-on

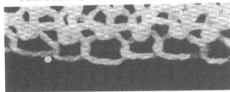

Make a slip knot, or crossed loop, on one needle, insert a second needle into this stitch, throw the yarn round it and pull through a loop. Place this new loop on the LHN. Repeat this action until you have the required number of stitches on the needle. Knit the first row into the **front** of the loops for a loopy cast-on row.

Cable Cast-on

Make a slip knot, or simply loop the yarn over one needle (Elizabeth Zimmermann's method). Place a second needle **behind** the slip knot or loop and pull through a loop. Place this new loop on the LHN. Now insert the RHN in the space **between** the two stitches and pull through a loop. Place this new loop on the LHN. Continue in this way until you have the number of stitches required.

Circular Cast-on

Cast on the number of stitches you wish to use, **plus one**, on one needle, using any of the methods discussed for flat knitting. Slip these stitches onto the number of needles needed for the circular knitting, with the stitches distributed as specified in the pattern. Join the stitches into a round by lifting the set of needles. Knit the first round plain, knitting the last cast-on stitch together with the first one.

Loop Cast-on (Tessa Lorant)

Take your knitting yarn and cross it to make a simple loop (not a knot), yarn tail to the left. Using one of the needles you will be knitting with, knit and purl alternately into the loop, as though you were knitting into an over of a previous row or round. Knit over the doubled yarn. Distribute the stitches on the needles, as above, and pull the yarn end. You need not pull it **tight** until you have knitted several rounds. This method is a great help for making a neat central start.

Crochet Chain Finish

Knit a round or row, plain or purl as appropriate for the pattern. Select a group of stitches with the crochet hook and crochet them all off together with a double crochet stitch. Now make a set of chain stitches. The number of stitches crocheted off together, and the number of chains crocheted between the sets of stitches, will vary with the original pattern and how you wish to finish it. Several crochet finishes are given as alternatives to the knitted finishes in some of the doily patterns.

Frill Cast-off
(Tessa Lorant)

Knit the first stitch to be cast off. *Yarn forward, **make** a stitch by slipping the RHN purlwise under the yarn bar between the first stitch, now on the RHN, and the second stitch, still on the LHN, and purl through a stitch. Draw the first (knitted), stitch over the second (purled), stitch, then **knit** the next stitch on the LHN, pso (cast off) and repeat from *. This will double the original number of stitches to be cast off.

This is one of my favourite cast-offs, which I worked out to overcome the problems of casting off on an outside curve; it simply is not adequate to use many of the other methods, and there are several bonuses. The extra length provided by doubling the stitches worked often produces a faint **frill**, from which I derived the name of the cast-off; the small holes, made by using the untwisted, raised 'bar' increase, not only add a lacy border to a delicate knitted fabric, they also provide attractive 'anchor loops' for a fringe. The loops are also useful for semi-grafting or latch-up.

Knitted Chain Cast-off
(Mary Medlam)

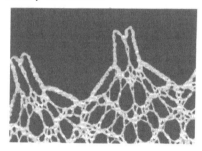

To make a knitted chain, slip a stitch or slip knot, as a base, onto the RHN. *Now, using the LHN, insert it through the loop on the RHN, from back to front (to make the quickest chain). Knit through another loop, using the RHN in the usual way. Repeat from * for as many sts as are required in the chain. (Ch6 means work a knitted chain consisting of 6 sts.) The knitted chains are interspersed with decreases and cast-offs appropriate to the pattern to make a cast-off row or round.

Looped Knitted Picot Chain
(Mary Medlam)

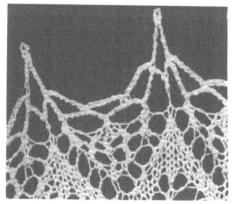

A looped knitted picot is made by working a chain, then working into the first stitch of the chain and pso.
You may wish to make a looped knitted picot in the centre of a knitted chain, often starting in the middle of a chain of a previous row or round. Knit into the first st of the knitted chain, pso; knit into the 2nd chain st and pso. Continue in this way until you come to the middle of the chain of the previous row or round. *Work half the number of chain required, make a looped knitted picot of appropriate size, pso, work the second half of the chain. Knit into the middle of the chain of the previous row or round, pso. Repeat from *.

SIDEWAYS KNITTED DOILIES

By far the easiest way to knit doilies is to knit them on two needles, joining the cast-on and cast-off selvedges at the end. The only disadvantage of this method is that the final join may show if it is done inexpertly, or if there is no readily imitated row to use for grafting. Here are one or two suggestions for overcoming this difficulty:

Making a Hidden Join:

(a) Use a variegated, or random-dyed yarn. The difference in the colourations detracts the eye from spotting the join. Even an expert can find it difficult to pinpoint precisely where such a join appears. This is, perhaps, the best method for inexperienced knitters. The resulting doiley is also unusual and combines the patterns of both stitch pattern and yarn colour pattern to give you pleasing and individual results.

(b) Use the **Open Loop Cast-on,** and graft the open loops of the last row to the open loops of the first row. This is an entirely successful method provided you not only know how to graft, but also know how to graft in pattern. It is crucial to graft in the background pattern being worked, whether this is garter stitch, stocking stitch, reversed stocking stitch, moss stitch or some of the more advanced lace grounds.

(c) Use the **Knitted Cast-on,** knitting into the front of the loops. This method leaves small, single loops to be semi-grafted onto later, so providing an easily 'graftable' edge for knitters new to this method of joining knitted selvedges.

(d) Cast on and off in the usual way and sew these two selvedges together. This is the simplest method, but it is also the most noticeable, however neatly it is done.

(e) Deliberately cast off every time a 'wedge' is knitted. Combine the knitted wedges by sewing, crocheting or embroidery.

Traditional Pattern:
Florinda Doily

𝕱LORINDA DOILY*

Materials: Silver Gauge Category: 'Fine Yarn'.
Pair of needles, sizes 2.00 mm – 2.75 mm (14s – 12s).

Illustrations: Coats Mercer Crochet 20; 2.00 mm (14s) needles.
South Maid random pink; pair of 2.75 mm (12s) and 4.00 mm (8s) needles.

Measurements: 19.5 cm (7.75 ins) diameter at widest points (page 15); weight 10g.
28 cm (11 ins) diameter at widest points; weight 20g.

This traditional pattern is a real delight for the beginner to knitting lace doilies. Knitted on two needles, the circular effect is produced by keeping some stitches 'in holding', so that the outside edge becomes very much longer than the inside edge. The doily is finished by connecting the cast-on and cast-off edges. The illustrated versions were semi-grafted, but see the **Techniques** section for other methods of joining.

The simple eyelet lace pattern is worked on a garter stitch base, making the doily reversible for a grafted or sewn join. The advantage of knitting doilies sideways is that the outside edge can readily be made with all kinds of serrated or other shaped finishes, no more difficult to knit than a sideways knitted lace edging.

The smaller doily is the original, traditional pattern. The larger doily (illustrated above) is made by replacing the first two stitches with O, K2tog on every EVEN row. Cast off the lace points by using a 4.00 mm (8s) needle where the instructions say C8.

Florinda Pattern

Lacy Version

Use a pair of needles and cast on 23 sts. Use the **Knitted Cast-on** for semi-grafting the cast-on and cast-off edges, or start with open loops for a grafted join. **Use a size 4.00 mm (8s) needle for the C8 cast-offs.**

Row   1: K20, O2, K2tog, K1   Row   2: O, K2tog, K1, P1, K19, U
Row   3: K23   Row   4: O, K2tog, K20, U
Row   5: K16, (O2, K2tog)2, O2, K2
Row   6: O, K2tog, K1, (P1, K2)2, P1, K15, U
Row   7: K25   Row   8 O, K2tog, K22, U
Row   9: K10, K2tog, O2, K2tog, K3, (O2, K2tog)3, K1
Row 10: O, K2tog, K1, P1, (K2, P1)2, K5, P1, K10, U
Row 11: K26   Row 12: C8, K16, U
Row 13: K14, O2, K2tog, K1   Row 14: O, K2tog, K1, P1, K13, U
Row 15: K17   Row 16: O, K2tog, K14, U
Row 17: K10, (O2, K2tog)2, O2, K2
Row 18: O, K2tog, K1, (P1, K2)2, P1, K9, U
Row 19: K19   Row 20: O, K2tog, K16, U
Row 21: K4, K2tog, O2, K2tog, K3, (O2, K2tog)3, K1
Row 22: O, K2tog, K1, (P1, K2)2, P1, K5, P1, K4, U
Row 23: K20   Row 24: C8, K10, (O, K2tog)6

Repeat Rows 1 - 24 nine times.
Join the cast-on and cast-off edges as unobtrusively as possible.

Traditional Version

Row   1: K20, O2, K2tog, K1   Row   2: K3, P1, K19, U
Row   3: K23   Row   4: K22, U
Row   5: K16, (O2, K2tog)2, O2, K2   Row   6: K3, (P1, K2)2, P1, K15, U
Row   7: K25   Row   8 K24, U
Row   9: K10, K2tog, O2, K2tog, K3, (O2, K2tog)3, K1
Row 10: K3, P1, (K2, P1)2, K5, P1, K10, U
Row 11: K26   Row 12: C8, K16, U
Row 13: K14, O2, K2tog, K1   Row 14: K3, P1, K13, U
Row 15: K17   Row 16: K16, U
Row 17: K10, (O2, K2tog)2, O2, K2   Row 18: K3, (P1, K2)2, P1, K9, U
Row 19: K19   Row 20: K18, U
Row 21: K4, K2tog, O2, K2tog, K3, (O2, K2tog)3, K1
Row 22: K3, (P1, K2)2, P1, K5, P1, K4, U
Row 23: K20   Row 24: C8, K10, (O, K2tog)6

Repeat Rows 1 - 24 nine times.
Join the cast-off and cast-on edges as unobtrusively as possible.
Time: Each set of 24 rows took approximately 15 minutes to knit.

$\mathbb{K}$LONDYKE DOILY

Materials	Silver Gauge Category: 'Fine Yarn'. Pair of needles, sizes 2.00 mm - 2.75 mm (14s - 12s).
Illustration:	Coats Mercer Crochet 20, random-dyed green. Pair of 2.00 mm (14s) needles.
Measurement:	25 cm (10 ins) diameter at the widest points; weight 15g.

Another traditional sideways knitted doily, perhaps even more attractive than **Florinda,** though very slightly more difficult to knit. The random-dyed yarn used for the illustrated version enhances the swirl effect of the central part of the doily. Though the join is semi-grafted, it is hard to spot.

It is important to dress the doily to display the picots surrounding the large scal-lops. This adds a lightness the doily would otherwise lack.

Always **knit** off the O2 of a previous row by knitting into the first part of the loop and dropping the second part. Always **(P1, K1)** into the O2 of the previous row whenever there is a P1 in the instructions.

Each pattern of 42 rows took approximately 30 minutes to knit.

Klondyke Pattern

Use a pair of needles and cast on 27sts. The **two** methods of working the O2 of the previous rows are emphasised in detail the first time only. Please see page 18.

Row 1: K24, O2, K2tog, K1
Row 2: O, K2tog, K1 into O2 of previous row, dropping second loop, K23, U
Row 3: K24, O2, K2   Row 4: O, K2tog, K24, U
Row 5: K24, O2, K2   Row 6: O, K2tog, K24, U
Row 7: K18, K2tog, O2, K2tog, K2, O2, K2
Row 8: O, K2tog, K5, (P1, K1) into O2 of previous row, K17, U
Row 9: K15, K2tog, O2, (K2tog)2, O2, K2tog, K1, O2, K2
Row 10: O, K2tog, K4, P1, K3, P1, K15, U
Row 11: K16, K2tog, O2, K2tog, K4, O2, K2
Row 12: O, K2tog, K7, P1, K16, U
Row 13: K13, K2tog, O2, (K2tog)2, O2, K2tog, K3, O2, K2
Row 14: O, K2tog, K6, P1, K3, P1, K13, U
Row 15: K14, K2tog, O2, K2tog, K6, O2, K2
Row 16: O, K2tog, K9, P1, K14, U
Row 17: K8, K2tog, O2, K2tog, K6, K2tog, O2, K2tog, K2, O2, K2
Row 18: O, K2tog, K5, P1, K9, P1, K8, U
Row 19: K5, K2tog, O2, (K2tog)2, O2, K2tog, K2, K2tog, O2, (K2tog)2, O2, K2tog, K1, O2, K2
Row 20: O, K2tog, K4, (P1, K3, P1, K5)2, U
Row 21: (K6, K2tog, O2, K2tog)2, K4, O2, K2
Row 22: O, K2tog, K7, P1, K9, P1, K6, U
Row 23: K3, K2tog, O2, (K2tog)2, O2, K2tog, K2, K2tog, O2, (K2tog)2, O2, (K2tog)2, O2, K2tog, K1
Row 24: O, K2tog, K4, P1, K3, P1, K5, (P1, K3)2, U
Row 25: K4, K2tog, O2, K2tog, K6, K2tog, O2, K2tog, K1, K2tog, O2, K2tog, K1
Row 26: O, K2tog, K5, P1, K9, P1, K4, U
Row 27: K8, K2tog, O2, K2tog, K5, K2tog, O2, K2tog, K1
Row 28: O, K2tog, K9, P1, K8, U
Row 29: K5, K2tog, O2, (K2tog)2, O2, K2tog, K2, K2tog, O2, K2tog, K1
Row 30: O, K2tog, K6, P1, K3, P1, K5, U
Row 31: K6, K2tog, O2, K2tog, K3, K2tog, O2, K2tog, K1
Row 32: O, K2tog, K7, P1, K6, U
Row 33: K3, K2tog, {O2, (K2tog)2}2, O2, K2tog, K1
Row 34: O, K2tog, K4, (P1, K3)2, U
Row 35: K4, K2tog, O2, K2tog, K1, K2tog, O2, K2tog, K1
Row 36: O, K2tog, K5, P1, K4, U
Row 37: K7, K2tog, O2, K2tog, K1   Row 38: O, K2tog, K8, U
Row 39: K5, K2tog, O2, K2tog, K1   Row 40: O, K2tog, K6, U
Row 41: K3, K2tog, O2, K2tog, K1   Row 42: O, K2tog, K5, (O, K2tog)10

Repeat rows 1 to 42 seven times (8 patterns in all).
Connect the cast-on and cast-off rows as unobtrusively as possible.

CATHERINE WHEEL DOILY

Materials: Silver Gauge Category 'Fine Yarn'.
Pair of needles, sizes 2.00 mm – 3.25 mm (14s – 10s).

Illustrations: Coats Mercer Crochet 20, cream; 2.75 mm (12)s needles.
South Maid cotton, old gold; 3.25 mm (10s) needles.

Measurements: Smaller Doily: 24 cm (9.5 ins) diameter at widest points; weight 15g.
Larger Doily: 36 cm (14 ins) diameter at widest points; weight 30g.

Though it looks quite intricate, this design is not too difficult to knit. The knitting pattern tries to imitate the many 'Point' lace patterns of pillow lace. Based on a knitted lace edging pattern, the central section is filled in by using 'stitches in holding', so making it possible to work a doily in flat knitting. The doily in the illustration has had the cast-off and cast-on edges joined by semi-grafting, but you can use any method you may prefer.

Just to prove that knitted lace doilies do not necessarily have to be worked in very fine yarns and needles, the larger design shows the doily worked on 3.25 mm (10s) needles, a size even beginners would not consider difficult to work with. Another advantage is that the size of the doily itself increases, without any further work. There is a slight pattern difference in the doilies; the smaller one has more lace spaces in the central section. This is the pattern given; replace Row 9 with the instructions in curly brackets for the larger version.

It is important to dress the doily so that each picot point is displayed. The centre of the large doily, illustrated on the inside front cover, has been filled with crochet, but you can leave a large hole or fill the centre in any way you choose.

Catherine Wheel Pattern (Tessa Lorant)

Using a pair of needles, cast on 30 stitches in the most appropriate manner for your eventual join with the cast-off edge. The illustration was worked using the **Knitted Cast-on.**

C'7 means cast off using the **Frill Cast-off.** It is very helpful to put a safetly pin into the 9th stitch from the beginning of the needle, denoting that this will be the **first** stitch to be knitted in pattern after the cast-off.

Row   1: K21,(O2,K2tog)4,K1
Row   2: O,K2tog,K1,P1,(K2,P1)3,K20,U (1 st left on RHN)
Row   3: K20,(O2,K2tog)6,K1
Row   4: O,K2tog,K1,(P1,K2)5,P1,K19,U (2 sts left on RHN)
Row   5: K19,(O2,K2tog)9,K1
Row   6: O,K2tog,K1,(P1,K2)8,P1,K18,U (3 sts left on RHN)
Row   7: K46
Row   8: O,K2tog,K43,U (4 sts left on RHN)
Row   9: K1,(O,K2tog)21,K2.....{K9,(O,K2tog)17,K2 for large doily}
Row 10: O,K2tog,K42,U (5 sts left on RHN)
Row 11: K17,K2tog,(K2,K2tog)6,K1
Row 12: C'7,(K2tog,K1)4,K2tog,K14,U (6 sts left on RHN)
Row 13: K15,(O2,K2tog)4,K1
Row 14: O,K2tog,K1,P1,(K2,P1)3,K14,U (7 sts left on RHN)
Row 15: K14,(O2,K2tog)6,K1
Row 16: O,K2tog,K1,(P1,K2)5,P1,K13,U (8 sts left on RHN)
Row 17: K13,(O2,K2tog)9,K1
Row 18: O,K2tog,K1,(P1,K2)8,P1,K12,U (9 sts left on RHN)
Row 19: K40
Row 20: O,K2tog,K37,U (10 sts left on RHN)
Row 21: K1,(O,K2tog)18,K2
Row 22: O,K2tog,K36,U (11 sts left on RHN)
Row 23: K11,K2tog,(K2,K2tog)6,K1
Row 24: C'7,(K2tog,K1)4,K2tog,K20

Repeat Rows 1 - 24 nine times (10 patterns in all) and cast off.
Alternatively, repeat Rows 1 - 24 eight times, then repeat Rows 1 - 23 once, C'7, then leave the rest of Row 24 to be grafted or semi-grafted.

DOILIES KNITTED 'IN THE ROUND'

Undoubtedly, one of the most successful ways of knitting lace doilies is 'in the round', that is using circular knitting. Not everyone is practised in this form of knitting, but several of the patterns given here, marked with * in the **Contents**, are simple enough for a beginner to try. Perhaps the most difficult part of this type of knitting is getting a neat start. You may find my method of starting with a loop helpful (see **Techniques**), because you need not tighten the loop completely until you have knitted a few rounds.

The number of needles used for circular knitting can vary. Knitters generally use a set of four needles; one to knit with and three to hold the stitches. However, some patterns are best worked on sets of five, six or even eight needles, depending on how the pattern is constructed. If you are knitting a large table centre, for example, you may like to change to more, rather than longer, needles after the first forty rounds. Alternatively, you may find a circular needle useful, if you can find one in the correct size.

As already mentioned in the **Introduction**, the finish for circular knitted doilies is traditionally done in crochet. Some knitters do not like to crochet, and they will find Mary Medlam's **Knitted Chain** and **Looped Knitted Picot** techniques very helpful when finishing their knitting in keeping with the pattern being worked.

Finish for Traditional Dahlia Doily Pattern

Work as for the **Dahlia Centre Pattern**, page 43, then continue as follows:

Round	51:	P*	Round	52:	P*
Round	53:	P*	Round	54:	P*
Round	55:	P*	Round	56:	P*
Round	57:	K*, increasing 2 stitches on each needle. (240 sts)			
Round	58:	K*	Round	59:	(O, K2tog)*
Round	60:	K*	Round	61:	(O, K2tog)*
Round	62:	K*	Round	63:	(O, K2tog)*
Round	64:	K*, increasing 4 stitches on each needle. (252 sts)			
Round	65:	P*	Round	66:	P*
Round	67:	P*	Round	68:	P*
Round	69:	P*	Round	70:	P*
Round	69:	K*	Round	72:	Cast off.

BUTTERFLY DOILY

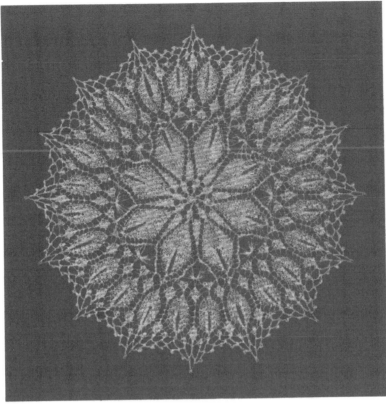

Materials: Silver Gauge Category: 'Very Fine Yarn'.
Set of 4 or 5 needles, 1.00 mm - 1.50 mm (18s - 16s).

Illustration: Coats Mercer Crochet 60, white.
Set of four 1.50 mm (16s) needles.

Measurement: 23 cm (9 ins) diameter at widest points; weight 12g.

This delicate little doily, designed by Mary Medlam, incorporates the 'butterfly stitch', which gives such a charming effect to the 'wings' surrounding the central lace. The flower petals surrounding the butterflies make a fitting finish to the knitting, and the extra round of picots after the chain finish gives a light and lacy look to the doily. You do not need to know how to crochet to give the doily a crochet finish look!

In order to bring out the full beauty of the looped knitted picots, pin each one out **through** its loop, and tension the knitting to its fullest extent, to achieve that attractively vandyked outline. You will find that, when the doily is thoroughly wetted, you need to use quite a lot of force to produce the required result. It is easier to pin the doily out, then leave it for an hour before moving the pins still further out.

Butterfly Pattern (Mary Medlam)

Use a set of 4 needles to cast on 8 sts, distributed 2, 2, 4 on three needles. You may prefer to distribute the stitches onto 4 needles, and knit with a 5th, after Round 18. Simply knit 22 stitches on Round 19, then bring in another needle to knit the remaining 22 sts from that needle.

All ODD rounds are K* unless otherwise directed in the pattern.

Round	2:	(O, K1)*
Round	4:	(O, K2tog)*
Round	5:	({K1, P1 into O of Round 4}, K1)*
Round	6:	(K1, O, K2)*
Round	7:	(K1, {K1, P1 into O of Round 6}, K2)*
Round	8:	(K2tog, O, SKtog, K1)*
Round	9:	(K1, {K1, P1, K1, P1 into O of Round 8}, K2)*
Round	10:	K*, + 1 At the end of each needle knit on 1 st from the next needle.

Round	12:	(O, K4, O, SK2tog)*
Round	14:	(K1, O, K4, O, K2)*
Round	16:	(K2, O, K4, O, K3)*
Round	18:	(K3, O, SKtog, K2tog, O, K4)*
Round	20:	(K4, O, K2, O, K5)*
Round	22:	(K5, O, K2tog, O, K6)*
Round	24:	(K6, O, K'1, O, K7)*
Round	26:	(K7, O, K'1, O, K8)*
Round	28:	(SKtog, K5, O, K3, O, K5, K2tog, P1)*

Round	29:	(K17, P1)*
Round	30:	(SKtog, K4, O, K2tog, O3, SK2tog, O, K4, K2tog, P1)*
Round	31:	(K7, {K1, P1, K1 into O of previous round}, K7, P1)*
Round	32:	(SKtog, K3, O, K2tog, K3, SKtog, O, K3, K2tog, P1)*
Round	33:	(K15, P1)*
Round	34:	(SKtog, K2, O, K2tog, K3, SKtog, O, K2, K2tog, P1)*
Round	35:	(K13, P1)*
Round	36:	(SKtog, K1, O, K2tog, K3, SKtog, O, K1, K2tog, P1)*
Round	37:	(K11, P1)*
Round	38:	(SKtog, O, K2tog, K3, SKtog, O, K2tog, P1)*
Round	39:	(K9, P1)*, + 1 (remember to count this as 1 of K9)
Round	40:	(O, K2tog, drop next 3 sts, unravel carefully to give 10 strands, O2; knit under the 10 strands, O2, SKtog, O, SK2tog)*
Round	41:	(K2, {K1, P1, K1, P1, K1 into the O2 of the previous round}, K1, repeat {-}, K3)*
Round	42:	(O, K15, O, K1)*
Round	43:	K*
Round	44:	(K2tog, O, K'1, O, SKtog, K1)*

Round 45: +1   Round 46: (O, K3, O, SK2tog)*
Round 48: (O, K5, O, K'1)*
Round 50: (K1, O, SKtog, K1, K2tog, O, K2)*
Round 52: (K2, O, SK'2tog, O, K3)*
Round 54: (K3, O, K'1, O, K4)*   Round 56: (K4, O, K'1, O, K5)*
Round 58: (SKtog, K3, O, K'1, O, K3, K2tog, P1)*

Round 59: (K11, P1)*
Round 60: (SKtog, K3, O, K'1, O, K3, K2tog, P1)*
Round 61: (K11, P1)*
Round 62: (SKtog, K2, O, K3, O, K2, K2tog, P1)*
Round 63: (K11, P1)*
Round 64: (SKtog, K1, O, K5, O, K1, K2tog, P1)*
Round 65: (K11, P1)*
Round 66: (SKtog, O, K1, O, SKtog, K1, K2tog, O, K1, O, K2tog, P1)*
Round 67: (K11, P1)*, +1   Round 68: (O, K3, O, SK2tog)*
Round 69: K*, +1, end Round with SK2tog

Finishing Rounds

Knitted Finish Round:
Round   1: Place last knitted st on RHN. (Ch7, SK2tog, pso)*
Round   2: Work to the centre of the first chain loop (see page 14, second paragraph
           of **Knitted Looped Picot Chain**). (Ch7, K into 3rd Ch, pso, Ch3,, K into
           middle of next Ch7 loop, pso)*.

Crochet Finish:
Round   1: Pick up last knitted st. (7 ch, 1 dc into next 3 sts)*.
Round   2: Ss to centre of Ch7, *7 ch, 1 ss into 3rd ch and take this through the other
           st, 3 ch, 1 dc into the centre of next Ch7 loop. Repeat from *.

SMALL MAT
Acanthus Leaf

TULIP DOILY*

Materials: Silver Gauge Category: 'Fine Yarn'.
Set of four needles, sizes 2.00 mm – 2.75 mm (14s – 12s).

Illustration: Coats Mercer Crochet 20, white.
Set of four 2.00 mm (14s) needles.

Measurement: 22 cm (9 ins) diameter at widest points; weight 15g.

    This is another delightful, but readily knitted, doily design by Mary Medlam. The 8-pointed central star is a traditional start to many circular doily patterns, and is always attractive. The star pattern branches out into lacy tulip shapes, the second set interspersed with tulip leaves. A delightful doily for spring. Why not try it in yellow for that sunny look?

    The chain finish can be worked using knitting needles or a crochet hook, whichever you prefer. Be sure to dress the doily corrrectly to display the attractive lace points to their full advantage.

Tulip Doily Pattern (Mary Medlam)

Use a set of 4 or 5 needles, cast on 8 stitches and distribute these 4, 2, 2 on three needles or 2 stitches on each of 4 needles.

All ODD rounds are K*, i.e. KNITTED PLAIN, but occasionally stitches are shifted from one needle to another. This is emphasised in the pattern.

Round	2: (O, K1)*		Round	4: (O, K2)*
Round	6: (O, K3)*		Round	8: (O, K4)*
Round	10: (O, K5)*		Round	12: (O, K6)*
Round	14: (O, SKtog, K5)*		Round	16: (O, K'1, O, SKtog, K4)*

Round 18: (O, K3, O, SKtog, K3)*
Round 20: (O, K2tog, O, K1, {O, SKtog}2, K2)*
Round 22: (O, K2tog, O, SK2tog, {O, SKtog}2, K1)*
Round 24: (O, K2tog, O, SK2tog, {O, SKtog}2)*
Round 26: ({O, K1}2, SK2tog, K1, O, K2)*
Round 28: (O, K3, O, SK2tog, O, K3)*
Round 30: (O, K5)*
Round 32: (O, K1, O, SKtog, K1, K2tog)*
Round 34: (O, K3, O, SK2tog)*
Round 36: (O, K5, O, K'1)*
Round 38: (K1, O, SKtog, K1, K2tog, O, K2)*
Round 40: (O, SKtog, O, K3, O, K2tog, O, K'1)*

Round 41: +1. At the end of each needle knit on 1 st from the next needle.
Round 42: (O, SKtog, O, K3, O, K2tog, O, SK2tog)*
Round 43: +1
Round 44: (O, SKtog, O, K3, O, K2tog, O, SK2tog)*
Round 45: +1
Round 46: ({K1, O}2, K3, {O, K1}2, SK2tog)*
Round 47: +1
Round 48: (O, K3, O, SK2tog)*

Round 50: (O, K5, O, K'1)*
Round 52: (O, K2tog)*
Round 54: (O, K2tog)*

Round 55: K*, K2tog

Finishing Round

Knitted Finish:
Place first st on RHN. (Ch5, K2tog, pso)*. (pso is equivalent to a one st cast-off.)

Crochet Finish:
Place hook in first st. *5 ch, 1 dc into next 2 sts. Repeat from *.

WINDMILL DOILY*

Materials: Silver Gauge Category: 'Fine Yarn'.
Set of 4 or 5 needles, sizes 2.00 mm – 2.75 mm (14s – 12s).

Illustrations: Coats Mercer Crochet 20, white.
Set of four or five 2.00 mm (14s) needles.

Measurement: 21 cm (8.25 ins) diameter at widest points; weight 10g.

The very lacy surround to this doily is shown off beautifully by the windmill 'sails' in stocking stitch fabric. An even tension in your knitting is essential here to display the design well. This is another relatively simple doily to knit, even for a beginner, yet it has enough charm to interest the more advanced knitter. The textures separating the lace spaces on the outer ring of the doily are a particularly effective foil for the lace, yet they are not difficult to knit. Be sure to smooth the stocking stitch sections carefully to enhance the contrast with the lace spaces and the textured panels.

The illustration is knitted in a combination of yarn and materials which should not cause any problems for the beginner. Advanced knitters can, of course, substitute the finest yarns and needles they can find. Treasure any old steel 16s, 18s or 20s you may have, and use them to make gossamer doilies using Coats Mercer Crochet 60, or even finer, yarns.

Windmill Pattern (Mary Medlam)

Use a set of 4 needles and cast on 8 stitches, distributed 3, 3, 2 on three needles. All ODD rounds are K*, i.e: KNITTED PLAIN, but occasionally stitches are shifted from one needle to another (abbreviation: + 1). This is emphasised in the pattern instructions.

If you prefer, distribute the needles 2, 2, 4 and introduce a fifth needle during, say, Round 19, knitting off half the stitches from the needle containing the double number.

Round 2: (O, K1)*	Round 4: (O, K2tog)*	
Round 6: (O, K2)*	Round 8: (O, K3)*	
Round 10: (O, K4)*	Round 12: (O, K5)*	
Round 14: (O, K2tog, O, K1, O, SKtog, K1)*		
Round 16: (O, K2tog, O, K3, O, SKtog)*		
Round 18: (O, K1, O, SKtog, O, SK2tog, O, K2tog)*		
Round 20: (O, K3, O, SKtog, K1, K2tog)*		
Round 22: (O, K5, O, SK2tog)*		
Round 24: (O, K8)*	Round 26: (O, K9)*	
Round 28: (O, K10)*	Round 30: (O, K11)*	
Round 32: (O, K12)*	Round 34: (O, K13)*	
Round 36: (O, K14)*	Round 38: (O, SKtog, K1, K2tog)*	
Round 40: (O, K1, O, SK2tog)*		
Round 42: (O, K3, O, K'1)*		
Round 44: (O, K1, SK2tog, K1, O, K'1)*		
Round 46: (O, K1, SK2tog, K1, O, K'1)*		
Round 48: (K2, O, K'1, O, K3)*		

Round 49: + 1. At the end of each needle take on one stitch from the next needle. Do this for all following ODD rows.

Round 50: (K2, O, K'1, O, K2, SK2tog)*
Round 52: (K2, O, K'1, O, K2, SK2tog)*
Round 54: (K1, O, K3, O, K1, SK2tog)*
Round 56: (O, K2, O, K'1, O, K2, O, SK2tog)*

Round 57: K*, + 1, SK2tog

Finishing Round

Knitted Finish:
Work on last stitch on RHN. Pso has the same effect as casting off 1 st.
{Ch6, K2tog, pso, Ch6, SK2tog, pso, Ch6, SKtog, pso, Ch6, SK2tog, pso}*

Crochet Finish:
1 dc into the last st of the final round. *6 ch, 1 dc in next 2 sts, 6 ch, 1 dc in next 3 sts, 6 ch, 1 dc in next 2 sts, 6 ch, 1 dc in next 3 sts. Repeat from * all round the doily.

CHEVRON TRACERY DOILY*

Materials: Silver Gauge Category: 'Fine Yarn'.
Set of 4 or 5 needles, sizes 2.00 mm - 2.75 mm (14s - 12s).

Illustration: Coats Mercer Crochet 20, white.
Set of four or five 2.75 mm (12s) needles.

Measurement: 28 cm (11 ins) diameter at widest points; weight 20g.

This very lacy doily is not difficult to make, even for a beginner to circular lace knitting. The illustration shows the doily worked in fairly, but not very, fine cotton, using a reasonably large needle size. Even so, the effect is delicate and charming. The design would be an excellent choice for a first effort at this type of knitting, but the doily is effective enough to be welcomed by the experienced knitter, too. Work it in finer yarn and with finer needles for a very delicate lace.

The relatively large size of the illustrated version makes it an excellent choice for a set of table mats, with matching table centre and dish stands. Work it in random-dyed cotton if you are a beginner and are afraid of an uneven tension. The random-dyed yarns produce attractive patterns in their own right, giving unusual effects.

Chevron Tracery Pattern (Mary Medlam)

Use a set of 4 needles and cast on 8 stitches, distributed 4, 2 and 2 on three needles.
All ODD rounds are K*, except where specified in the pattern.

Round   2: (O, K1)*   Round   4: (O , K3, O, K'1)*
Round   6: (O, K2, O, SKtog, K1, O, K'1)*
Round   8: (K1, O, SKtog, K1, K2tog, O, K2)*
Round 10: (K2, O, SK2tog, O, K3)*   Round 12: (K3, O, K'1, O, K4)*
Round 14: (K4, O, K'1, O, K5)*   Round 16: (O, K5, O, K'1)*
Round 18: (K1, O, SKtog, K1, K2tog, O, K2)*
Round 20: (O, K2, O, K3, O, K1, K2tog)*
Round 22: (K1, K2tog, O, K'1, O, SK2tog, O, K'1, O, SKtog)*

Round 23: +2 (At the end of each needle knit on 2 sts from the next needle.)
Round 24: (O, K3, O, K'1, O, K3, O, SK2tog)*
Round 26: (O, K2tog, O, K'1, O, SKtog, O, K'1)*
Round 28: (K2tog, O, K3, O, SKtog, K1)*

Round 29: +1   Round   30: (O, K5, O, SK2tog)*
Round 32: (O, K1, K2tog, O, K'1, O, SKtog, K1, O, K'1)*
Round 34: (O, K1, K2tog, O, K3, O, SKtog, K1, O, K'1)*
Round 36: (K1, K2tog, O, K5, O, SKtog, K2)*
Round 38: (K2tog, O, K7, O, SKtog, K1)*

Round 39: +1
Round 40: (O, K2, K2tog, O, K'1, O, SKtog, K2, O, SK2tog)*
Round 42: (O, K2, K2tog, O, K3, O, SKtog, K2, O, K'1)*
Round 44: (O, K2, K2tog, O, K2, O, SKtog, K1, O, SKtog, K2, O, K'1)*
Round 46: (K2, K2tog, O, K'1, O, SKtog, K1, K2tog, O, K'1, O, SKtog, K3)*
Round 48: (K1, K2tog, O, K'1, O, SKtog, O, SK2tog, O, K2tog, O, K'1, O, SKtog, K2)*
Round 50: (K2tog, O, K'1, {O, SKtog}2, K1, {K2tog, O}2, K'1, O, SKtog, K1)*

Round 51: +1
Round 52: (O, K'1, {O, SKtog}2, O, SK2tog, O, {K2tog, O}2, K'1, O, SK2tog)*
Round 53: K*, +1, finish Round SK2tog

Finishing Round

Knitted Finish Round: (pso is equivalent to casting off one st)
Place last knitted stitch on RHN. ({Ch6, SKtog, pso}3; K1, pso; K2tog, pso; {Ch6, K2tog, pso}2; Ch6, SK2tog, pso)*.

Crochet Finish Round:
1 dc into last st of Round 53, *(6 ch, 1 dc into next 2 sts)3, 1 dc in next st, 1 dc in next 2 sts, (6 ch, 1 dc into next 2 sts)2, 6 ch, 1 dc into next 3 sts)*. Optional 2nd round of chain.

ERRY-GO-ROUND DOILY*

Materials: Silver Gauge Category: 'Very Fine Yarn'.
Set of four needles, sizes 1.50 mm – 2.00 mm (16s – 14s).

Illustration: Coats Mercer Crochet 40, white.
Set of four 1.50 mm (16s) needles.

Measurement: 17.5 cm (7 ins) diameter at widest points; weight 10g.

This dainty little doily is still well within the beginner's scope. The illustrated doily was worked on the finer 40s cotton, with the finest needles still available, 1.50 mm (16s). Even this size is now being phased out, making it hard to work really fine knitted laces.

You can, of course, use thicker yarns and larger needle sizes to make larger, less dainty doilies. However, knitting with fine yarn and needles when working a relatively simple pattern gives good practice for attempting the more intricate designs in this book, and working those in the fine yarns.

As with all the doilies, it pays to take the trouble to dress the finished doily carefully, both to bring out its ornamental edging, and to display the knitted lace pattern to its best advantage.

Merry-go-round Pattern (Mary Medlam)

Use a set of 4 needles and cast on 8 stitches, distributed 2, 2, 4 on three needles. All ODD rounds are K*, i.e. KNITTED PLAIN, but occasionally stitches are shifted from one needle to another (abbreviation: + 6). This is emphasised in the pattern directions.

Round   2: (O, K 1)*
Round   4: (O, K 3, O, K'1)*
Round   6: (O, K 5, O, K'1)*
Round   8: (O, K 7, O, K'1)*
Round 10 (O, SK tog, K 2 tog, O, K'1)*
Round 12: (K 1, O, K 2 tog, O, K 3, O, SK tog, O, K 2)*
Round 14: (K 2, O, K'1, O, K 3)*
Round 16: (K 3, O, K'1, O, K 4)*
Round 18: (K 4, O, K'1, O, K 5)*
Round 20: (K 5, O, K'1, O, K 6)*
Round 22: (O, K 5, SK 2 tog, K 5, O, K'1)*
Round 24: (K 1, O, K 4, SK 2 tog, K 4, O, K 2)*
Round 26: (O, SK tog, O, K 3, SK 2 tog, K 3, O, K 2 tog, O, K'1)*
Round 28: (K 1, O, SK tog, O, K 2, SK 2 tog, K 2, O, K 2 tog, O, K 2)*
Round 30: (O, K 2, O, SK tog, O, K 1, SK 2 tog, K 1, O, K 2 tog, O, K 2, O, K'1)*
Round 32: (O, K 4, O, SK tog, O, SK 2 tog, O, K 2 tog, O, K 4, O, K'1)*
Round 34: (O, K 6, O, SK tog, K 1, K 2 tog, O, K 6, O, K'1)*
Round 36: (O, K 8, O, SK 2 tog, O, K 8, O, K'1)*
Round 38: (O, K 10, O, K'1)*

Round 39: + 6. At the end of each needle take on 6 sts from the next needle.
Round 40: (O, K 5, SK 2 tog, K 5)*
Round 42: (O, K 1, O, K 4, SK 2 tog, K 4)*
Round 44: (O, K 3, O, K 3, SK 2 tog, K 3)*
Round 46: (O, K 2 tog, O, K'1, O, SK tog, O, K 2, SK 2 tog, K 2)*
Round 48: (O, K 2 tog, O, K 3, O, SK tog, O, K 1, SK 2 tog, K 1)*
Round 50: (O, K 2 tog, O, K 2 tog, O, K'1, O, SK tog, O, SK tog, O, SK 2 tog)*

Round 51: K*

Finishing Round

Knitted Finish: (pso is equivalent to casting off one st)
Put the last knitted stitch on the RHN. {(Ch6, K 2 tog, pso)2, Ch6, SK 2 tog, pso, (Ch6, SK tog, pso)2, Ch6, K 1, pso}*

Crochet Finish:
Slip the last knitted stitch onto a crochet hook. *6 ch, 1 dc into next 2 sts)2, 6 ch, 1 dc into next 3 sts, (6 ch, 1 dc in next 2 sts)2, 6 ch, 1 dc into next stitch. Repeat from * all round the doily.

NORTH STAR DOILY

Materials: Silver Gauge Category: 'Fine Yarn'.
Set of five needles, sizes 1.50 mm – 2.00 mm (16s – 14s).

Illustration: Coats Mercer Crochet 20, white.
Set of five 1.75 mm (15s), and a pair of 1.50 mm (16s), needles.

Measurement: 29 cm (11.5 ins) diameter at widest; weight 30g (including edging).

This is a basic traditional 8-pointed star pattern, and very easy to work. There is very little lace knitting until the edging pattern, just the contrast of the lace space outlines for the double eight-pointed star. The rest of the pattern consists of stocking stitch, moss stitch and garter stitch - all three stitch patterns readily worked by any beginner. The **Wicker Edging,** page 62, gives an attractive finish to the doily.

North Star Pattern

Use a set of 5 needles and cast on 8 stitches, distributed 2, 2, 2, 2 on four needles. All EVEN rounds are K* until Round 35, which will be emphasised in the pattern. After this, knit moss stitch between the star points, i.e. where you knitted plain on the previous round you knit purl, and vice versa.

Round	1: K*	Round	3: (O, K 1)*
Round	5: (O, K 2)*	Round	7: (O, K 3)*
Round	9: (O, K 4)*	Round	11: (O, K 5)*
Round	13: (O, K 6)*	Round	15: (O, K 7)*
Round	17: (O, K 8)*; (72 sts)	Round	19: (O, K 1, O, K 2tog, K 6)*
Round	21: (O, K 3, O, K 2tog, K 5)*	Round	23: (O, K 5, O, K 2tog, K 4)*
Round	25: (O, K 7, O, K 2tog, K 3)*	Round	27: (O, K 9, O, K 2tog, K 2)*
Round	29: (O, K 11, O, K 2tog, K 1)*	Round	31: (O, K 13, O, K 2tog)*; (128)
Round	33: O, K 1, O, K 2tog, K 13)*		
Round	35: (O, K 1, P1, K 1, O, K 2tog, K 12)*		

Round 36: (K 1, P1, K 1, P1, K 14)*
Round 37: (O, K 2, P1, K 2, O, K 2tog, K 11)*
Round 38: (K 2, P1, K 1, P1, K 14*
Round 39: (O, K 1, {P1, K 1}3, O, K 2tog, K 10)*
Round 40: ({K 1, P1}4, K 12)*
Round 41: (O, K 2, {P1, K 1}2, P1, K 2, O, K 2tog, K 9)*
Round 42: (K 2, {P1, K 1}3, P1, K 12)*
Round 43: (O, K 1, {P1, K 1}5, O, K 2tog, K 8)*
Round 44: ({K 1, P1}6, K 10)*
Round 45: (O, K 2, {P1, K 1}4, P1, K 2, O, K 2tog, K 7)*
Round 46: (K 2, {P1, K 1}5, P1, K 10)*
Round 47: (O, K 1, {P1, K 1}7, O, K 2tog, K 6)*
Round 48: ({K 1, P1}8, K 8)*
Round 49: (O, K 2, {P1, K 1}6, P1, K 2, O, K 2tog, K 5)*
Round 50: (K 2, {P1, K 1}7, P1, K 8)*
Round 51: (O, K 1, {P1, K 1}9, O, K 2tog, K 4)*
Round 52: ({K 1, P1}10, K 6)*
Round 53: (O, K 2, {P1, K 1}8, P1, K 2, O, K 2tog, K 3)*
Round 54: (K 2, {P1, K 1}9, P1, K 6)*
Round 55: (O, K 1, {P1, K 1}11, O, K 2tog, K 2)*
Round 56: ({K 1, P1}12, K 4)*
Round 57: (O, K 2, {P1, K 1}10, P1, K 2, O, K 2tog, K 1)*
Round 58: (K 2, {P1, K 1}11, P1, K 4)*
Round 59: (O, K 1, {P1, K 1}13, O, K 2tog)*
Round 60: + 1 (at the end of each needle, knit on one st fom the next needle), ({K 1, P1}14, K 2)*, {K 1, P1}14, K 1

Round	61: (O, K 2tog, {K 1, P1}13, K 2)*	Round	62: K* (240 sts)
Round	63: ({K 1, K'1} in next st, K 29)*		
Round	64: P*	Round	65: P*
Round	66: P*	Round	67: ({K, K'1} in next st, K 30)*
Round	68: (O, K 2tog)*	Round	69: K* (64 sts on each needle)
Round	70: P*		
Round	71: {P1, K'1} in 1st st, P* (65, 64, 64, 64 = 257 sts)		
Round	72: P*	Round	73: K*

Surround the doily with the **Wicker Edging**, page 62.

TUFTED STAR DOILY

Materials: Silver Gauge Category: 'Fine Yarn'.
Set of four needles, sizes 1.50 mm – 2.00 mm (16s – 14s).

Illustration: Coats Mercer Crochet 20, white.
A set of four 2.00 mm (14s) needles.

Measurement: 28 cm (11 ins) diameter at widest pts; weight 20g (including edging).

This unusual pattern has an embossed surface, not often seen in doilies. Consequently, it has yet another decorative factor, apart from the lace fabric and the design. It does take a little more time to knit this doily, but the result is delightful and well worthwhile.

This traditional pattern is surrounded by a matching edging design which repeats the 'tufts' of the central section. The edging pattern has distinctive lace points with large eyelet lace spaces. Be careful to dress them to show up to their full advantage.

Tufted Star Pattern

Use a set of 4 needles and use the **Cable Cast-on** for 6 sts, distributed 2, 2, 2 on three needles. K* all ODD rounds except Round 3 and after Round 27. Always use the first st

36

on LHN as base for the 3-st tuft cast-ons, then purl back on these 4 sts. P3so means draw the 3 purled sts over the purled base st. It's easier to draw the sts over one by one.

Round 2: K*

Round 3: (O, K1)*

Round 4: K*

Round 6: (K1, O)*

Round 8: (K1, O, K3, O)*

Round 10: (K1, O, K2, c3, P4, P3so, K2, O)* (using fist st on LHN as base for cast-on)

Round 12: (K1, O, K2tog, K3, K2tog, O)*

Round 14: (K1, O, K2, c3, P4, P3so, K1, c3, P4, P3so, K2, O)*

Round 16: (K1, O, K2tog, K5, K2tog, O)*

Round 18: (K1, O, K1, {K1, c3, P4, P3so}2, K1, K2tog, O, K1, O)*

Round 20: (K1, O, K2tog, K6, O, K3, O)*

Round 22: (K1, O, K1, {K1, c3, P4, P3so}2, K1, K2tog, O, K2, c3, P4, P3so, K2, O)*

Round 24: (K1, O, K2tog, K6, O, K2tog, K3, K2tog, O)*

Round 26: (K1, O, K2, {c3, P4, P3so, K1}2, K2tog, O, K1, {K1, c3, P4, P3so}2, K2, O)*

Round 27: (P1, K17)*

Round 28: (P2, O, K2tog, K6, O, K2tog, K3, K2tog, O, P1)*

Round 29: (P2, K15, P1)*

Round 30: (O, K1, O, P2, O, K2, {c3, P4, P3so, K1}2, K2tog, O, K2, c3, P4, P3so, K2, O, P2)*

Round 31: K3, P2, K15, P2)*

Round 32: (O, K3, O, P3, O, K2tog, K6, O, K2tog, K1, K2tog, O, P3)*

Round 33: (K5, P3, K13, P3)*

Round 34: (O, K5, O, P4, O, K2, {c3, P4, P3so, K1}2, K2tog, O, K3tog, O, P4)*

Round 35: (K7, P4, K11, P4)*

Round 36: (K2tog, K3tog, K2tog; put these 3 sts back on LHN and K3tog, P2, O, K1, O, P2, O, K2tog, K5, K2tog, O, P2, O, K1, O, P2)*

Round 37: (P3, K3, P2, K9, P2, K3, P2)*

Round 38: (P3, O, K3, O, P3, O, K1, {K1, c3, P4, P3so}2, K2, O, P3, O, K3, O, P2)*

Round 39: (P3, K5, P3, K9, P3, K5, P2)*

Round 40: (P3, O, K5, O, P4, O, K2tog, K3, K2tog, O, P4, O, K5, O, P2)*

Round 41: (P3, {K7, P4}2, K7, P2)*

Round 42: (O, K1, O, P2; K2tog, K3tog, K2tog, put these 3 sts back on LHN and K3tog, P2, O, K1, O, P2, O, K2, c3, P4, P3so, K2, O, P2, O, K1, O, P2; K2tog, K3tog, K2tog, put these 3 sts back on LHN and K3tog, P2)*

Round 43: K3, P5, K3, P2, K7, P2, K3, P5)*

Round 44: (O, K3, O, P5, O, K3, O, P3, O, K2tog, K1, K2tog, O, P3, O, K3, O, P5)*

Round 45: (K5, P5, {K5, P3}2, K5, P5)*

Round 46: (O, K5, O, P5, O, K5, O, P4, O, K3tog, O, P4, O, K5, O, P5)*

Round 47: (K7, P5, K7, P4, K3, P4, K7, P5)*

Round 48: ({K2tog, K3tog, K2tog, put these 3 sts back on LHN and K3tog, P5}2, K1, P5; K2tog, K3tog, K2tog, put these 3 sts back on LHN and K3tog, P5)*

Round 49: P*

Round 50: P* (144 sts).

Cast off, or keep stitches on needles for knitting in the **Burr Edging**, page 61.

37

LATTICE STAR DOILY*

Materials: Silver Gauge Category: 'Very Fine Yarn'.
Set of four needles, sizes 1.50 mm – 2.00 mm (16s – 14s).

Illustration: Coats Mercer Crochet 40, white.
Set of four 1.50 mm (16s) needles.

Measurement: 23 cm (9 ins) diameter at widest pts; weight 15g (including edging).

This enchanting traditional doily is one of the simplest to make in circular knitting. If you do not feel confident about joining the edging to the doily, just make fringes through the **Frill Cast-off** loops.

The central, six-sided star is divided again into a further, larger star, with the space between points filled by an attractive lattice lace. The edging used to finish the doily has small lace points underlined by a chevron of 'true' knitted lace, that is single bars of the knitting yarn.

The knitted edging has been knitted **onto** the completed doily in the illustration, so making a join entirely in keeping with the knitting. The cast-on and cast-off edges have been semi-grafted and the join is not too obtrusive. Graft it for a completely invisible join.

Lattice Star Pattern

Use a set of 4 needles and cast on 3 sts, distributed (1, 1, 1) on three needles. **KNIT** the first and every other ODD round, unless otherwise directed in the pattern.

Round   2: (O, K 1)*
Round   4: (O, K 1)*
Round   6: (O, K 2)*
Round   8: (O, K 3)*
Round 10: (O, K 4)*
Round 12: (O, K 5)*
Round 14: (O, K 6)*
Round 16: (O, K 7)*
Round 18: (O, K 8)*
Round 20: (O, K 1, O, SK tog, K 6)*
Round 22: (O, K 3, O, SK tog, K 5)*
Round 24: (O, K 5, O, SK tog, K 4)*
Round 26: (O, K 7, O, SK tog, K 3)*
Round 28: (O, K 9, O, SK tog, K 2)*
Round 30: (O, K 11, O, SK tog, K 1)*
Round 32: (O, K 13, O, SK tog)*
Round 34: (O, SK tog, K 13, O, K 1)*

Round 35: K*, – 2. Knit to within 2 st at the end of each needle and transfer to next needle.
Round 36: O, K 1, O, K 2tog, O, SK tog, K 12)*
Round 38: (O, K 1, {O, K 2tog}2, O, SK tog, K 11)*
Round 40: (O, K 1, {O, K 2tog}3, O, SK tog, K 10)*
Round 42: (O, K 1, {O, K 2tog}4, O, SK tog, K 9)*
Round 44: (O, K 1, {O, K 2tog}5, O, SK tog, K 8)*
Round 46: (O, K 1, {O, K 2tog}6, O, SK tog, K 7)*
Round 48: (O, K 1, {O, K 2tog}7, O, SK tog, K 6)*
Round 50: (O, K 1, {O, K 2tog}8, O, SK tog, K 5)*
Round 52: (O, K 1, {O, K 2tog}9, O, SK tog, K 4)*
Round 54: (O, K 1, {O, K 2tog}10, O, SK tog, K 3)*
Round 56: (O, K 1, {O, K 2tog}11, O, SK tog, K 2)*
Round 58: (O, K 1, {O, K 2tog}12, O, SK tog, K 1)*
Round 60: (O, K 1, {O, K 2tog}13, O, SK tog)*

Round 61: K*
Round 62: Cast off using the **Frill Cast-off.**

You can either finish this doily by knotting a fringe through each picot produced by the **Frill Cast-off,** or you can surround the doily by knitting on the **Zigzag Edging,** page 60. Alternatively, make the edging with a small picot side selvedge and graft it to the picot loops of the **Lattice Star** centre.

$\mathcal{P}$HEASANT'S EYE DOILY

Materials: Silver Gauge Categories: 'Fine Yarn', 'Very Fine Yarn'.
Set of four needles, sizes 1.75 mm – 2.75 mm (15s – 12s).
Pair of needles, sizes 1.00 mm – 1.50 mm (18s – 16s).

Illustration: Doily: Coats Mercer Crochet 20, white.
Set of four 2.00 mm (14s) needles.
Lace Edging: Coats Mercer Crochet 40, white.
Pair of 1.50 mm (16s) needles.

Measurement: Doily: 24 cm (9.5 ins) diameter; weight 25g.
Plus edging at widest points: 31 cm (12 ins). Edging weight 10g.

This very attractive doily, traditionally used for a cake stand, is illustrated here surrounded by an attractive knitted lace edging discovered in an 1840s periodical by Miss Hetty Carr. The original had a number of errors, and only 10 lace spaces to each lace point. I have adapted the pattern to provide 15 lace spaces, and it is shown here worked in a finer yarn and needle size than the doily, to provide a dainty edging.

The edging starts with six stitches only, making it easy to graft the start and end rows, using any of the methods described in the **Techniques** section. The illustrated edging has been attached to the doily by threading a needle with the 20s crochet cotton, slipping it first through the picot loop of the doily, then over the picot edge loop of the edging. As each lace point has only 12 picot edges, and each doily design has 16 stitches, be sure to take up **two** doily picots at regular intervals to ensure a symmetric finish to the doily.

Pheasant's Eye Doily Pattern

Use a set of 4 needles, cast on 16 sts, and distribute them 5, 5, 6 on three needles. Note that occasionally the first stitch in the **ROUND** is **knitted**, then placed on the previous needle making it the **last** stitch in the round (- 1).

Round 1: K*	Round 2: K*
Round 3: K*	Round 4: (O3, K2)8
Round 5: ({K1, P1, K1, P1, K1, P1, K1} in O3 of previous round, K2)8
Round 6: K72
Round 7: K*; - 1. (Slip last st of rd onto next needle, to become 1st st of next rd.)
Round 8: (K9, O)8	Round 9: K80
Round 10: (K9, O, K1, O)8	Round 11: K96
Round 12: (K3, SK2tog, K3, O, K3, O)8	Round 13: K96
Round 14: (K2, SK2tog, K1, O, K2, O, SK2tog, O, K1, O)8
Round 15: K96
Round 16: (K1, SK2tog, {K1, O, K3, O}2)8	Round 17: K112
Round 18: (SK2tog, O, K1, O, SK2tog, O, K3, O, SK2tog, O, K1, O)8
Round 19: K112	Round 20: P112
Round 21: (P14, O)8	Round 22: P120
Round 23: (P5, O)24	Round 24: P144
Round 25: (P48, O)3	Round 26: K147
Round 27: (K2, K2tog, O, K1, O, K2tog)21	Round 28: K147
Round 29: (K4, O, K1, O, K2tog)21	Round 30: K168
Round 31: (K5, O, K1, O, K2tog)21	Round 32: K189
Round 33: (K6, O, K1, O, K2tog)21	Round 34: K210
Round 35: (K7, O, K1, O, K2tog)21	Round 36: K231
Round 37: K3, (O, K11)20, O, K7; - 1	Round 38: K252
Round 39: (K4, O, K1, O, K4, SK2tog)21	Round 40: K252
Round 41: K1; - 1; ({K3, O}2, K3, SK2tog)21
Round 42: K252
Round 43: K1; - 1; (K2, O, K1, O, SK2tog, O, K1, O, K2, SK2tog)21
Round 44: K252
Round 45: K1; - 1; (K1, {O, K3, O, K1}2, SK2tog)21
Round 46: K294
Round 47: K1; - 1; (O, K1, O, SK2tog, O, K3, O, SK2tog, O, K1, O, SK2tog)21
Round 48: K294
Round 49: (K2, O, K3, O, SK2tog, {O, K3}2)21
Round 50: K336

Cast off using the **Frill Cast-off.** Work the **Abaris Point Edging** (page 63) and attach it to the doily in any way you like.

ᴅAHLIA CENTRE

Materials: Silver Gauge Category: 'Fine Yarn'.
Set of four needles, sizes 1.50 mm – 2.00 mm (16s – 14s).

Illustration: Coats Mercer Crochet 20, white.
Set of four 1.50 mm (16s) needles and 2.00 mm (14s) needles.

Measurements: Knitted on 1.50 mm (16s) needles: 15.5 cm (6.25 ins) diameter;
Knitted on 2.00 mm (14s) needles: 19 cm (7.25 ins) diameter.

    This delightful traditional design can be used as the base for all kinds of table mats or doilies. The design is illustrated here and on page 58, worked on both 1.50 mm (16s) and 2.00 mm (14s) needles, the former with a narrow, easily made lace edging, the latter with a much wider edging which needs considerable shaping to provide a good surround for the central pattern. The latter design is large enough to form a table centre, or even a complete cover for a small table. The traditional **Dahlia Doily** is illustrated on page 6, showing the traditional reverse stocking stitch ridges.

    Permutations on the design are only dependent on the number of suitable knitted edging patterns in your possession. Many of the edgings given in my **Knitted Lace Edgings** (Thorn, 1981) can be used to provide you with several variations using this delightful traditional **Dahlia Centre.**

Dahlia Pattern

Using a set of 4 needles, cast on 6 stitches, distributed 2, 2, 2 on three needles. K* the first and all ODD rounds unless otherwise instructed in the pattern.

Round   2: (O, K1)*
Round   4: (O, K1)* (24 sts)
Round   6: (O, K3, O, K1)*
Round   8: (O, K5, O, K1)*
Round 10: (O, K7, O, K1)*
Round 12: (O, K9, O, K1)*
Round 14: (O, K11, O, K1)* (28, 28, 28 = 84 sts)
Round 16: ({O, K1}2, O, K2, K2tog, SKtog, K1, K2tog, {O, K1}3)*
Round 18: (O, K2, O, K3, O, K3tog, SK2tog, O, K3, O, K2, O, K1)*
Round 20: (O, K3, O, K1, O, {SKtog, K1, K2tog}2, O, K1, O, K3, O, K1)*
Round 22: (O, K4, O, K3, O, K3tog, SK2tog, O, K3, O, K4, O, K1)*
Round 24: (O, K5, O, K1, O, {SKtog, K1, K2tog}2, O, K1, O, K5, O, K1)*
Round 26: (O, K6, O, K3, O, K3tog, SK2tog, O, K3, O, K6, O, K1)*
Round 28: (K5, K2tog, O, K1, {O, SKtog, K1, K2tog}2, O, K1, O, SKtog, K6)*
Round 30: (K4, K2tog, O, K3, O, K3tog, O, K1, O, SK2tog, O, K3, O, SKtog, K5)*
Round 32: (K3, K2tog, O, K1, O, SKtog, K1, K2tog, O, K3, O, SKtog, K1, K2tog, O, K1, O, SKtog, K4)*
Round 34: (K2, K2tog, O, K3, O, K3tog, {O, K1, O, SK2tog}2, O, K3, O, SKtog, K3)*
Round 36: (K1, K2tog, O, K1, O, SKtog, K1, K2tog, {O, K1, O,K2tog}2, O, K1, O, SKtog, K1, K2tog, O, K1, O, SKtog, K2)*
Round 38: (K2tog, O, K3, O, K3tog, {O, K1, O, K2tog, O, K1, O, SK2tog}2, O, K3, O, SKtog, K1)*

Round 39: + 1. At the end of each needle, knit on 1 st from the following needle.
Round 40: (O, K1, O, SKtog, K1, K2tog, O, K1, O, K2tog, {O, K1, O, SK2tog}2, O, K1, O, K2tog, O, K1, O, SKtog, K1, K2tog, O, K1, O, SK2tog)*
Round 42: (O, {K2tog}3, O, K1, O, K2tog, {O, K1, O, SK2tog}3, O, K1, O, K2tog, O, K1, O, {SKtog}3, O, K1)*
Round 44: (K1, K3tog, O, K1, O, K2tog, {O, K1, O, SK2tog}4, O, K1, O, K2tog, O, K1, O, SK2tog, K2)*
Round 46: (K2tog, O, K1, O, K2tog, {O, K1, O, SK2tog}5, O, K1, O, K2tog, O, K1, O, SKtog, K1)*

Round 47: + 1 (68, 68, 68 = 204 sts)
Round 48: (O, K1, O, K2tog, {O, K1, O, SK2tog}6, O, K1, O, K2tog, O, K1, O, SK2tog)*
Round 50: (K6, {M', K12}5, M', K6)* (234 stitches, 78 on each needle)

Cast off, using the **Frill Cast-off.** Pull out the picots and use them to anchor a simple fringe. Alternatively, sew or knit on a lace edging of your choice. The **Spider Edging** (page 64), illustrated here and on page 6, is a very suitable one.

COMET DOILY

Materials: Silver Gauge Category: 'Fine Yarn'.
2 sets of four 1.50 mm – 2.00 mm (16s – 14s) needles, 1 short set and 1 long set.

Illustration: Coats Mercer Crochet 20, white.
2 sets of four 2.00 mm (14s) needles, 25 cm & 35 cm long.

Measurement: 38 cm (15 ins) diagonal on octagon; weight 30g (including edging).

Though the doily starts, as several others in this book do, with the simple 8-star pattern, it branches out into a lacy star shape, giving movement to the design. The idea of movement is increased by the lacy herringbone effect of the pattern surrounding the star. The doily is completed by a very simple edging.

I have dressed this doily into an octagonal shape, just to show that it is not always essential to make doilies circular. If you prefer it circular, simply pin it out on a circle.

This design, though it looks like a substantial table centre and might seem difficult to the novice to knitting, is actually very simple to knit and can readily be worked by the average knitter. The only problem lies at the join of the needles. Substitute a circular needle instead of a set of long 2.00 (14s) to make the knitting easier, and to avoid the tendency towards an uneven tension at the needle joins.

Comet Doily Pattern

Cast on 8 sts, using the short set of needles, and distributing them 3, 3, 2. Knit these 8 stitches.

K* all ODD rounds to Round 60.

Round	2:	(O, K 1)*	Round	4:	(O, K 2)*
Round	6:	(O, K 3)*	Round	8:	(O, K 4)*

Round   2: (O, K 1)*   Round   4: (O, K 2)*
Round   6: (O, K 3)*   Round   8: (O, K 4)*
Round 10: (O, K 5)*   Round 12: (O, K 6)*
Round 14: (O, K 7)*   Round 16: (O, K 8)*
Round 18: (O, K 1, O, SKtog, K 6)*   Round 20: (O, K 3, O, SKtog, K 5)*
Round 22: (O, K 2, O, SKtog, K 1, O, SKtog, K 4)*
Round 24: (O, K 2, {O, SKtog}2, K 1, O, SKtog, K 3)*
Round 26: (O, K 2, {O, SKtog}3, K 1, O, SKtog, K 2)*
Round 28: (O, K 2, {O, SKtog}4, K 1, O, SKtog, K 1)*
Round 30: (O, K 2, {O, SKtog}5, K 1, O, SKtog)*
Round 32: ({O, SKtog}7, O, K 2)*   Round 34: (K 1, {O, SKtog}6, O, K 4)*
Round 36: ({O, SKtog}6, O, K 6)*   Round 38: (K 1, {O, SKtog}5, O, K 8)*
Round 40: ({O, SKtog}5, O, K 10)*   Round 42: (K 1, {O, SKtog}4, O, K 12)*
Round 44: ({O, SKtog}4, O, K 14)*   Round 46: (K 1, {O, SKtog}3, O, K 16)*
Round 48: ({O, SKtog}3, O, K 18)*   Round 50: (K 1, {O, SKtog}2, O, K 20)*
Round 52: ({O, SKtog}2, O, K 22)*   Round 54: (K 1, O, SKtog, O, K 24)*
Round 56: (O, SKtog, O, K 26)*   Round 58: (K 1, O, K 28)*

Round 59: K* (240 sts)   Round 60: P*
Round 61: P*   Round 62: P*
Round 63: (K 3, Kfb)* (300 sts)   Round 64: (O, K 2tog)*
Round 65: (O, K 2tog)*   Round 66: (O, K 2tog)*
Round 67: (O, K 2tog)*   Round 68: (O, K 2tog)*
Round 69: (O, K 2tog)*   Round 70: (O, K 2tog)*

Round 71: K 1, (O, SKtog)*. There will be an odd stitch left at the end of each needle. Slip it, yarn forward (O), and take first st off next needle. Psso this st, then start on next needle. (Always knit the O of previous round and slip the knitted st.) Do this for Rounds 72 - 75 also.

Round 72: K 1, (O, SKtog)*   Round 73: K 1, (O, SKtog)*
Round 74: K 1, (O, SKtog)*   Round 75: K 1, (O, SKtog)*
Round 76: (O, K 2tog)*   Round 77: (O, K 2tog)*
Round 78: (O, K 2tog)*   Round 79: (O, K 2tog)*
Round 80: (O, K 2tog)*   Round 81: (K 7, Kfb)*, K 12 (336 sts)
Round 82: P*   Round 83: P*
Round 84: P*

Keep the open loops on the set of needles, or a circular needle, and knit them in with the **Cat's Eye Edging**, page 59.

TABLE SETS

Here are two enchanting table set designs, either of which would do justice to the finest glass and china. Both are illustrated worked in Coats Mercer Crochet 40, and on 1.50 mm (16s) needles, but of course you can choose coarser or finer yarn or needles.

The knitted finishes on the table centres are particularly attractive, but you will only display these centres at their best if you take particular trouble with dressing them. Be sure to pin out each picot carefully, and starch the piece sufficiently to keep the lace in shape.

Acanthus Leaf Table Centre

CHINESE LANTERN SET

Materials: Silver Gauge Category: 'Very Fine Yarn'.
Set of four 1.50 mm – 2.00 mm (16s – 14s) needles.

Illustration: Coats Mercer Crochet 40, white.
Set of four 1.50 mm (16s) needles.

Measurements: SMALL MAT: 14 cm (5.5 ins) diameter at pts; weight 5g. (Page 50)
MEDIUM MAT: 22 cm (8.75 ins) diameter at points; weight 12g.
TABLE CENTRE: 34 cm (13.5 ins) diameter at points; weight 25g.
(Title Page)

Mary Medlam's delicate design is ethereal even when worked in Mercer Crochet 40. If you are an experienced knitter you can use Mercer Crochet 60, or an even finer yarn, for an extremely fine lace. Be sure to dress the lace carefully, pulling it out to its full size, to display the pattern properly. The knitted finish for this set is particularly effective. The pattern is not too difficult to be attempted by the keen knitter.

If you wish to use your table set quite frequently, you might consider embedding your mats in plastic resin, so making heat-proof table mats.

MEDIUM MAT

Use a set of 4 needles and cast on 8 sts, distributed 2, 2 and 4 on three needles.

Round	1:	K*. Work all ODD rounds K* unless otherwise directed in the pattern.
Round	2:	(O, K1)*
Round	4:	(O, K3, O, K'1)*
Round	6:	(O, K2tog, O, K'1, O, SKtog, O, K'1)*
Round	8:	(K1, O, SKtog, O, K'1, O, K2tog, O, K2)*
Round	10:	(K2, O, SKtog, O, K'1, O, K2tog, O, K3)*
Round	12:	(K3, O, SKtog, O, K'1, O, K2tog, O, K4)*
Round	14:	(K1, K2tog, O, K1, O, SKtog, K1, K2tog, O, K1, O, SKtog, K2)*
Round	16:	(K2tog, O, K3, O, SK2tog, O, K3, O, SKtog, K1)*
Round	17:	+ 1. At the end of each needle knit on 1 st from the next needle.
Round	18:	(O, K2tog, O, K1, O, SKtog, O, K'1, O, K2tog, O, K1, O, SKtog, O, SK2tog)*
Round	20:	(O, K2tog, O, K3, O, SKtog, O, K'1)*
Round	22:	(K1, O, SKtog, O, SK2tog, O, K2tog, O, K2)*
Round	24:	(K2, O, SKtog, K1, K2tog, O, K3)*
Round	26:	(K3, O, SK2tog, O, K4)*
Round	28:	(O, SKtog, K2, O, K'1, O, K2, K2tog, O, K'1)*
Round	30:	(K1, O, SKtog, K5, K2tog, O, K2)*
Round	32:	(O, SKtog, O, SKtog, K3, {K2tog, O}2, K'1)*
Round	34:	(O, K2tog, O, K1, O, SKtog, K1, K2tog, O, K1, O, SKtog, O, K'1)*
Round	36:	(O, K2tog, O, K3, O, SK2tog, O, K3, O, SKtog, O, K'1)*
Round	38:	(O, K2tog, O, K5, O, K'1, O, K5, O, SKtog, O, K'1)*
Round	40:	(O, K2tog, O, K7, O, K'1, O, K7, O, SKtog, O, K'1)*
Round	41:	+ 1.
Round	42:	(SKtog, O, SKtog, K3, K2tog, O, K3, O, SKtog, K3, K2tog, O, K2tog, SK2tog)*
Round	44:	(O, SKtog, O, SKtog, K1, {K2tog, O}2, K'1)*
Round	46:	(K1, O, SKtog, O, SK2tog, O, K2tog, O, K2)*
Round	47:	+ 1.
Round	48:	(O, K2tog, O, K3, O, SKtog, O, SK2tog)*
Round	50:	(K2tog, O, K5, O, SKtog, K1)*
Round	51:	+ 1.
Round	52:	(O, K7, O, SK2tog)*
Round	54:	(O, K2, K2tog, O, K1, O, SKtog, K2, O, K'1)*
Round	56:	(K2, K2tog, O, K3, O, SKtog, K3)*
Round	58:	(K1, K2tog, O, K2tog, O, K'1, {O, SKtog}2, K2)*
Round	60:	(K2tog, O, K1, O, SKtog, O, K'1, O, K2tog, O, K1, O, SKtog, K1)*
Round	61:	+ 1.
Round	62:	(O, SK2tog, O, SKtog, K1, K2tog, {O, SK2tog}2)*
Round	63:	K*

Finishing Rounds

Knitted Finish:

Round 64: Pick up the last knitted stitch. ({Ch6, SK2tog, pso}3, Ch6, K1, pso)*.

Round 65: Knit into the first chain that you made, cast off 1 stitch; knit into 2nd chain made, cast off one st, knit into third chain made, cast off one stitch. This brings you to the middle of the 6 chain loop. ({Ch6, knit under next Ch6 loop, pso}3, Ch8, knit into 4th chain, pso, Ch4, knit under the next Ch6 loop, pso)*.

Crochet Finish:

8 ch crochet picot: 8 ch, 1 ss into 4th ch, 4 ch, 1 dc into next loop.

Place the last knitted stitch on a 1.00 mm crochet hook.

Round 1: *(6 ch, 1 dc into next 3 sts)3, 6 ch, 1 dc into next st. Repeat from *, then slip stitch to centre of next loop.

Round 2: *(8 ch, 1 dc into next loop)3, one 8 ch picot into next loop. Repeat from *.

SMALL MAT

Use the instructions given for the **MEDIUM MAT**, up to and including Round 35. Continue as follows:

Round 36: (K2tog, O, K3, O, SK2tog, O, K3, O, SKtog, K1)*

Round 37: K*, + 1, but finish round with SK2tog.

Finishing Rounds

Knitted Finish:

A Ch6 knitted picot chain = Ch6, knit into 3rd chain, pso, Ch3.

Round 38: Pick up the last knitted stitch. (Ch6, SK2tog, pso, Ch6, SKtog, pso, Ch6, K1, pso, Ch6, SKtog, pso, Ch6, SK2tog, pso, Ch6, SK2tog, pso)*.

Round 39: Knit into first chain made, cast off one st; knit into second chain made, cast off one st; knit into third chain made, cast off 1 st. This will bring you to middle of the first Ch6 loop. ({Ch6, knit under the next Ch6 loop, pso)2, make a Ch6 knitted picot chain, knit under next loop, pso, {Ch6, knit under next loop, pso}3)*.

Crochet Finish:

6 ch crochet picot: 6 ch, ss into 3rd ch, 3 ch, 1 dc in next loop.

Place the last knitted stitch on a 1.00 mm crochet hook.

Round 1: *6 ch, 1 dc into the following set of sts: 3, 2, 1, 2, 3, 3. Repeat from *. Ss to the middle of the next loop.

Round 2: (6 ch, 1 dc into next 2 loops, 1 6 ch picot, 1 dc into next loop, 6 ch, 1 dc into next 3 loops.

SMALL MAT
Chinese Lantern Pattern

LARGE MAT (Table Centre)

Follow the instructions given for the **MEDIUM MAT,** up to and including Round 59. Continue as follows, working K* for all ODD rows unless otherwise specified.

Round 60: ({K2tog,O}2,K3,{O,SKtog}2,K1)*

Round 61: + 1.
Round 62: (O,K2tog,O,K5,O,SKtog,O,SK2tog)*
Round 64: (O,K2tog,O,K7,O,SKtog,O,K'1)*
Round 66: (K2tog,O,K2,K2tog,O,K'1,O,SKtog,K2,O,SKtog,K1)*

Round 67: + 1.
Round 68: (O,K2,K2tog,O,K3,O,SKtog,K2,O,SK2tog)*
Round 70: (K2,{K2tog,O}2,K'1,{O,SKtog}2,K3)*
Round 72: (K1,K2tog,O,K1,O,SKtog,O,K'1,O,K2tog,O,K1,O,SKtog,K2)*
Round 74: (K2tog,O,K3,O,SKtog,O,K'1,O,K2tog,O,K3,O,SKtog,K1)*

Round 75: + 1.
Round 76: (O,K5,O,SKtog,O,K'1,O,K2tog,O,K5,O,SK2tog)*
Round 78: (O,K7,O,SKtog,O,K'1,O,K2tog,O,K7,O,K'1)*
Round 80: (K1,O,SKtog,K3,K2tog,O,K2tog,SK2tog,SKtog,O,SKtog,K3,K2tog, O,K2)*
Round 81: K*

Repeat the instructions given for the **MEDIUM MAT** from, and including, Round 44 onwards. Use the same finishing instructions.

ACANTHUS LEAF SET

Materials: Silver Gauge Category: 'Very Fine Yarn'.
Set of four 1.00 mm - 1.50 mm (18s - 16s) needles.

Illustration: Coats Mercer Crochet 40, white.
Set of four 1.50 mm (16s) needles.

Measurements: SMALL MAT: 17 cm (6.50 ins) diameter; weight 5g. (Page 25.)
MEDIUM MAT: 25 cm (10 ins) diameter; weight 12g.
TABLE CENTRE: 36 cm (14 ins) diameter; weight 20g. (Page 46.)

This superb set of table mats is shown here worked in Coats Mercer Crochet 40, and on 1.50 mm (16s) needles. The table centre has a particularly gossamer look, though in fact neither the yarn nor the needle size are particularly fine. A more advanced design, it is well worth the effort to make these delicate laces - they will add grace to any special table setting. Though it looks delicate, knitted lace is quite robust, provided the yarn used is of high quality. It is false economy to buy inexpensive yarns for articles which could well become treasured family heirlooms.

The design can be used to make small, medium or large circular mats. The size can, of course, be further adjusted by using different combinations of yarn and needles.

Acanthus Leaf Patterns (Mary Medlam)

MEDIUM MAT

Use a set of 4 needles and cast on 8 stitches, distributed 2, 2 and 4 on three needles.

Round   1: K*   Round 2: (O, K1)*

Round   3: K*   Round 4: K*

Round   5: (O, K1)*   Round 6: K*

Round   7: K*   Round 8: K*

Round   9: (K2tog, O2, SKtog)*

Round 10: (K1, {K1, P1 into O2 of previous round}, K1)*

Round 11: (O, K2tog, O2, SKtog)*

Round 12: (K2, {K1, P1 into O2 of previous round}, K1)*

Round 13: (K1, K2tog, O2, SKtog)*

Round 14: (K2, {K1, P1 into O2 of previous round}, K1)*

Round 15: (K1, K2tog, O2, SKtog)*

Round 16: (K2, {K1, P1 into O2 of previous round}, K1)*

Round 17: (Drop the 1st stitch, leaving 6 straight yarn bars, {O, K1} under the 6th yarn bar, so catching all the bars in a loop, O, SKtog, K2tog)*

Round 18: ({K1, P1, K1, P1, K1} into O of previous round, K1, {K1, P1, K1, P1, K1} into O of previous round, K2tog)*

Round 19: K*. **Work all ODD rounds to Round 51 K*.**

Round 20: (O, K4, SK2tog, K4, O, K'1)*

Round 22: (K1, O, K3, SK2tog, K3, O, K2)*

Round 24: (O, SKtog, O, K2, SK2tog, K2, O, K2tog, O, K1)*

Round 26: (K1, O, SKtog, O, K1, SK2tog, K1, O, K2tog, O, K2)*

Round 28: ({O, SKtog}2, O, SK2tog, {O, K2tog}2, O, K1)*

Round 30: (K1, {O, SKtog}2, O, K'1, {O, K2tog}2, O, K2)*

Round 32: ({O, SKtog}3, K1, {K2tog, O}3, K1)*

Round 34: (K1, {O, SKtog}2, O, SK2tog, {O, K2tog}2, O, K2)*

Round 36: (K2, {O, SKtog}2, O, K1, {O, K2tog}2, O, K3)*

Round 38: (K2tog, O, K1, {O, SKtog}2, K1, {K2tog, O}2, K1, O, SKtog, K1)*

Round 39: + 1. (At the end of each needle knit on 1 st from the next needle)

Round 40: (O, K3, O, SKtog, O, SK2tog, O, K2tog, O, K3, O, SK2tog)*

Round 42: (K5, O, SKtog, O, K1, O, K2tog, O, K6)*

Round 44: (O, SKtog, K1, K2tog, O, K1)*

Round 46: (K1, O, SK2tog, O, K2)*

Round 48: (K2, O, K'1, O, K3)*

Round 50: (K2tog, O, K3, O, SKtog, K1)*

Round 51: K*, + 1

Round 52: (O, K2, P1, K2, O, SK2tog)*

Round 53: (K3, P1, K4)*

Round 54: (O, K3, P1, K3, O, K'1)*

Round 55: (K4,P1,K5)*
Round 56: (O,K2,K2tog,P1,SKtog,K2,O,K'1)*
Round 57: (K4,P1,K5)*
Round 58: (O,K2,K2tog,P1,SKtog,K2,O,K'1)*
Round 59: (K4,P1,K5)*
Round 60: (O,K2,K2tog,P1,SKtog,K2,O,K'1)*
Round 61: (K4,P1,K5)*
Round 62: (O,K2,K2tog,P1,SKtog,K2,O,K'1)*
Round 63: (K4,P1,K5)*
Round 64: (K1,O,K1,K2tog,P1,SKtog,K1,O,K2)*
Round 65: (K4,P1,K5)*
Round 66: (O,SKtog,O,K2tog,P1,SKtog,O,K2tog,O,K1)*
Round 67: (K4,P1,K5)*
Round 68: (K1,O,SKtog,O,SK2tog,O,K2tog,O,K2)*

Round 69: K*. **Work all following ODD rounds K*.**
Round 70: ({O,SKtog}2,K1,{K2tog,O}2,K1)*
Round 72: (K1,O,SKtog,O,SK2tog,O,K2tog,O,K2)*
Round 74: ({O,SKtog}2,K1,{K2tog,O}2,K1)*
Round 76: (K1,O,SKtog,O,SK2tog,O,K2tog,O,K2)*
Round 78: ({O,SKtog}2,K1,{K2tog,O}2,K1)*
Round 80: (K1,O,SKtog,O,SK2tog,O,K2tog,O,K2)*
Round 81: K*

Finishing Round

Knitted Finish:
Pick up last st knitted, (Ch7, K2tog, pso, Ch7, K2tog, pso, K1, pso, K2tog, pso, Ch7, K2tog, pso, Ch7, K1, pso)*.

Crochet Finish:
Slip last knitted stitch into crochet hook. *(7 ch, 1 dc into next 2 sts)2, 1 dc into next st, 1 dc into next 2 sts, 7 ch, 1 dc into next 2 sts, 7 ch, 1 dc into next st. Repeat from * to the end of the round.

SMALL MAT
Follow the direction given for the **Medium Mat** up to, and including, Round 41.
Continue as follows:

Round 42: (O, K2tog, O, K1,{O, SKtog}2, K1,K2tog, O, K2tog, O, K1, O, SKtog, O, K'1)*
Round 43: K*
Round 44 (O, K2tog, O, K3, O leaving 6 yarn bars, O, K1 under the O, SKtog, O, K'1)*

Round 45: K*
Round 46: ({K2tog, O}2, K1, {O, SKtog}2, K1)*
Round 47: K*, +1
Round 48: (O, K2tog, O, K3, O, SKtog, O, SK2tog)*
Round 49: K*

Optional:
Round 50: ({K2tog, O}2, K1, {O, SKtog}2, K1)*
Round 51: K*, +1
Round 52: (O, K2tog, O, K3, O, SKtog, O, SK2tog)*
Round 53: K*

Finishing Rounds for SMALL MAT:
Knitted Finish:
Pick up the last knitted stitch. ({Ch7, K2tog, pso}2, Ch7, K1, pso)*

Crochet Finish:
Pick up last knitted st. *Ch7, 1 dc into the following set of sts: 2, 2, 1. Repeat from *.

TABLE CENTRE
This design starts in the same way as the two previous ones, but 14 rounds are inserted after Round 29, and then the design is continued, starting again with Round 19.

Round 30: (K1, {O, SKtog}2, K1, {K2tog, O}2, K2)*
Round 31: K*
Round 32: ({O, SKtog}2, O, SK2tog, O, {K2tog, O}2, K1)*
Round 33: K*
Round 34: (K1, {O, SKtog}2, K1, {K2tog, O}2, K2)*
Round 35: – 3. **Knit to within three stitches of the end of each needle and transfer these stitches to the next needle.**
Round 36: (O, SK2tog, O2, {SKtog, O}2, SK2tog, O, K2tog)*
Round 37: (K2, {K1, P1 into O of previous round}, K7)*
Round 38: (O, K1, O, K2tog, O2, SKtog, O, K1, O, SKtog, K1, K2tog)*
Round 39: (K4, {K1, P1 into O of previous round}, K7)*
Round 40: (O, K2tog, K1, K2tog, O2, SKtog, K1, SKtog, O, SK2tog)*
Round 41: (K4, {K1, P1 into O of previous round}, K5)*
Round 42: (O, K2tog, K1, K2tog, O2, SKtog, K1, SKtog, O, K'1)*
Round 43: (K4, {K1, P1 into O of previous round}, K5)*
Round 44: (K2tog, drop next st, leaving 6 yarn bars, O, K1 under the 6th bar, O, SKtog, K2tog, drop next st, leaving 6 yarn bars, O, K1 under the 6th bar, O, SKtog, K1)*
Round 45: +1 **before starting to knit.**
({K1, P1, K1, P1, K1 into O of previous round}, K1, {K1, P1, K1, P1, K1 into O of previous round}, K2tog, {K1, P1, K1, P1, K1 into O of previous round}, K1, {K1, P1, K1, P1, K1 into O of previous round}, SK2tog)*
Continue by starting again with Round 19 of the **MEDIUM MAT.** Finish as for this mat.

KNITTED LACE EDGINGS

Many traditional doily patterns have central sections worked in circular knitting, finishing with rather plain, unserrated outlines. These pieces were traditionally edged with an appropriate lace edging, worked sideways.

The advantage here is that all kinds of interesting and varied outlines can be made for the same doily centre, giving a much greater choice of lace finish. The disadvantage is that the join, when worked by simply sewing the cast-on and cast-off edges together, shows fairly obviously.

As with the sideways knitted doilies, the join can be relatively simply disguised by using the methods given in the **Techniques** section, or by considering the points raised in the discussion about **Sideways Knitted Doilies,** on page 15.

One very interesting use of lace edgings is to make a cake frill. This is nothing more than the combination of a 'straight' and a 'curved' lace edging, but it can make a delightful ornament for your favourite-size cake. Make several in different sizes and colours, and you will never be at a loss on how do decorate a special cake. Your friends will love the idea, and think you wonderfully clever!

Do adapt any favourite lace edging pattern you may already have and give yourself the opportunity to combine various doily centres with different lace edgings.

I have grouped all the lace edging designs together here, so that you can use them in any way you wish. The patterns for the doilies which use lace edgings mention which particular edging was used to make the doily illustrated with the pattern instructions.

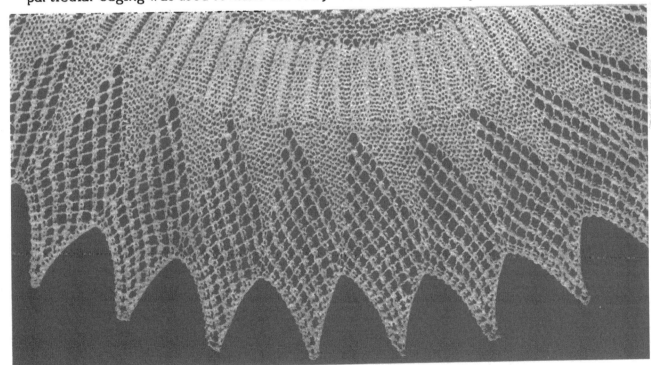

Shark's Tooth Edging

ESTIVE CAKE FRILL

Materials: Silver Gauge Category: 'Fine Yarn'.
Pair of needles, sizes 1.50 mm – 2.00 mm (16s – 14s).

Illustration: Twilley's Forty, white.
Pair of 1.50 mm (16s) needles.

Measurements: Height: 5 cm (2 ins). Depth of border: 6 cm (2.25 ins) to points.
Cake surround: 21.5 cm (8.5 ins) diameter. Weight: 23g.

This delightful frill for any cake is really quite simple to make. It is nothing more than the combination of two lace edgings, a straight one to surround the cake and a curved one to add a doily effect. Starch the completed lace sufficiently to stand on its own, place the cake on a suitable base and simply place the cake frill over it. Make yourself several in different sizes and colours, for different occasions. The knitting is not too advanced, and if you are not yet up to a virtually invisible join, just cover the join with a bow of festive ribbon!

Remember that, in order to get a matching latch-up, your total number of picots must be the same. You will also find that latching up right or wrong sides together makes a difference. The straight lace has 6 picots, the curved lace has 5 picots. The illustrated frill used 30 straight, and 36 curved, lace pattern repeats, 180 picots each.

Cake Frill Pattern

STRAIGHT LACE

Use a pair of needles and cast on 16 sts, in whichever way is appropriate to the join you intend to use. The illustrated frill used a **Knitted Cast-on**.
Foundation Row: K*

Row   1: O2, K2tog, K4, P6, K3, Kbf
Row   2: K17, dropping extra loop of last st.
Row   3: O2, (K2tog)2, O2, K2tog, K6, K2tog, O2, K2tog, Kbf
Row   4: K4, P1, K1, P6, K2, P1, K3
Row   5: O2, K2tog, K4, (O, K2tog)3, K5, Kbf
Row   6: K7, P6, K6
Row   7: O2, (K2tog)2, O2, K2tog, K1, (O, K2tog)2, K1, K2tog, O2, (K2tog)2, K1
Row   8: K4, P1, K1, P6, K2, P1, K3
Row   9: O2, K2tog, K4, (O, K2tog)3, K4, K2tog
Row 10: K5, P6, K6
Row 11: O2, (K2tog)2, O2, K2tog, K6, K2tog, O2, K3tog
Row 12: K2, P1, K9, P1, K3

Repeat Rows 1 - 12 for the required length. Each pattern repeat took 8 minutes to knit.

CURVED LACE

Use a pair of needles and cast on 26 stitches in an appropriate way. A **Knitted Cast-on** was used for the illustrated frill.

Row   1: O2, K2tog, (K2, O, K2tog)2, P10, K4, O, K2
Row   2: O, K2tog, K17, (O, K2tog, K2)2, dropping extra loop on last st
Row   3: O2, K2tog, (K2, O, K2tog)2, K13, O, K2tog, O, K2
Row   4: O, K2tog, K6, P10, K1, U
Row   5: Sk, (O, K2tog)5, K2, (O, K2tog)2, O, K2
Row   6: O, K2tog, K7, P10, (K2, O, K2tog)2, K2
Row   7: O2, K2tog, (K2, O, K2tog)2, K1, (O, K2tog)4, K2, (O, K2tog)3, O, K2
Row   8: O, K2tog, K8, P10, K1, U
Row   9: Sk, (O, K2tog)5, K1, (K2tog, O)3, K2tog, K1
Row 10: O, K2tog, K7, P10, (K2, O, K2tog)2, K2
Row 11: O2, K2tog, (K2, O, K2tog)2, K12, (K2tog, O)2, K2tog, K1
Row 12: O, K2tog, K6, P10, K1, U
Row 13: Sk, P10, K3, K2tog, O, K2tog, K1
Row 14: O, K2tog, K17, (O, K2tog, K2)2
Row 15: O2, K2tog, (K2, O, K2tog)2, P10, K4, K2tog, K1
Row 16: O, K2tog, K16, (O, K2tog, K2)2

Repeat Rows 1 - 16 for required length. Each pattern repeat took 10 minutes to knit.

SHARK'S TOOTH EDGING

Materials: Silver Gauge Category: 'Fine Yarn'.
Pair of 1.75 mm - 2.50 mm (15s - 11s) needles.

Illustration: Coats Mercer Crochet 20.
Pair of 2.00 mm (14s) needles.

The deep 'Shark's Teeth' make an eye-catching finish to any round doily centre. The pattern illustrated here is used round the **Dahlia Centre**.

Shark's Tooth Pattern

Use the first st of the next round as a base for casting on 28 sts, ready for knitting the edging in with the open loops.

Rows ending in 'K2tog, U' should be worked by knitting together the first stitch of the border and the appropriate centre stitch.

Foundation Row: P27, K2tog (using first st from centre).

Row 1: K14, (O, K2tog)6, O, K2
Row 2: K16, P10, U
Row 3: K12 (O, K2tog)6, O, K2
Row 4: K17, P10, K2, K2tog
Row 5: K16, (O, K2tog)6, O, K2
Row 6: K18, P10, U

58

Row	7: P10,K4,(O,K2tog)6,O,K2	Row	8: K31,K2tog
Row	9: K3,P10,K5,(O,K2tog)6,O,K2	Row	10: K30,U
Row	11: P10,K6,(O,K2tog)6,O,K2	Row	12: K33,K2tog
Row	13: K20,(O,K2tog)6,O,K2	Row	14: K22,P10,U
Row	15: K18,(O,K2tog)6,O,K2	Row	16: K23,P10,K2,K2tog
Row	17: K22,(O,K2tog)6,O,K2	Row	18: K24,P10,U
Row	19: P10,K10,(O,K2tog)6,O,K2	Row	20 K37,K2tog
Row	21: K3,P10,K11,(O,K2tog)6,O,K2	Row	22: K36,U
Row	23: P10,K26	Row	24: C11,K26,K2tog

Repeat until all the stitches are worked off the centre needles, ending last row C38 or, if you prefer to semi-graft, C11,K26,K3tog.

CAT'S EYE EDGING*

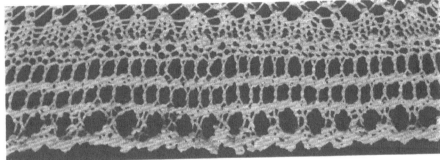

Illustration: Coats Mercer Crochet 20, white.
Pair of 2.00 mm (14s) needles.

This very simple edging can be worked by any beginner, and is not difficult to join unobtrusively.

Cat's Eye Pattern

Using a pair of 2.00 mm (14s) needles, and the last stitch of the last round as a base, cast on 8 sts.
Foundation Row: P7,P2tog.

Row	1: K2,(O,K2tog)2,O2,K2
Row	2: K3,P5,K1,K2tog
Row	3: K2,(O,K2tog)2,K4
Row	4: C2,K1,P4,K1,K2tog

Repeat this simple 4-row pattern until all the loops of the centre are taken up. The illustration on page 44 shows the cast-on and final row loops of the edging semi-grafted.
If you wish to make the edging separately, simply replace the Foundation Row with P8 and replace the K1,K2tog endings on Rows 2 and 4 with K2.

ZIGZAG EDGING*

Materials: Silver Gauge Category: 'Very Fine Yarn'.
Pair of needles, sizes 1.50 mm – 2.00 mm (16s – 14s).

Illustration: Coats Mercer Crochet 40, white.
Pair of 1.50 mm (16s) needles.

Zigzag Pattern

Working **clockwise** round the outer edge of the doily, attach the edging by knitting the **last** stitch of each odd row **together with** the picot loop of the doily. You may find it convenient to pull out, say, 20 picots at a time and have them on a spare needle. Use the same size needles as used for the doily centre and cast on 15 sts in whichever way is appropriate for your method of connecting the cast-on and cast-off edges.

Row   1: K6, K2tog, O, K4, O, K2tog, K2tog (knitting last stitch with picot loop)
Row   2: (K3, O, K2tog)2, K1, K2tog, O2, K2
Row   3: K3, P1, K1, K2tog, O, K6, O, K2tog, K2tog
Row   4: K3, O, K2tog, K2, K2tog, O, K1, (K2tog, O2)2, K2
Row   5: K3, P1, K2, P1, (K3, O, K2tog)2, K2tog
Row   6: K3, O, (K2tog)2, O, K11
Row   7: C3, K8, O, K2tog, K1, O, K2tog, K2tog
Row   8: K3, O, K2tog, K1, O, K2tog, K7

Repeat Rows 1 – 8 as needed, or until the **Lattice Star Doily** is completely surrounded.

Burr Edging

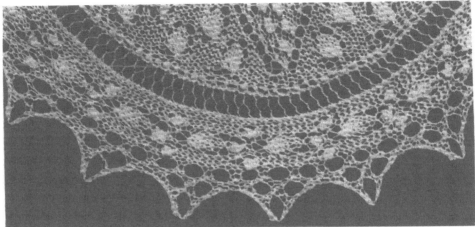

Materials: Silver Gauge Category: 'Fine Yarn'.
Pair of needles, sizes 1.50 mm – 2.00 mm (16s – 14s).

Illustration: Coats Mercer Crochet 20, white.
Pair of 2.00 mm (14s) needles.

Burr Edging Pattern

Cast on 15 sts for the edging. The doily illustrated on page 36 was worked by knitting the pattern **onto** the open loops of the centre, using the last stitch of the last round as the foundation stitch for the cast-ons.

Foundation Row: K14, K2tog (knitting together one st from last doily round and last st of edging)

Row 1: K3, O, K2tog, K1, P2, O, K1, O, P2, K1, O2, K2tog, K1
Row 2: K3, P1, K3, P3, K5, O, (K2tog)2 (using 1 st from centre for 2nd K2tog)
Row 3: K3, O, K2tog, K1, P2, O, K3, O, P2, K5
Row 4: K7, P5, K5, O, (K2tog)2
Row 5: K3, O, K2tog, K1, P2, O, K5, O, P2, K1, (O2, K2tog)2
Row 6: (K2, P1)2, K3, P7, K5, O, (K2tog)2
Row 7: K3, O, K2tog, K1, P2; K2tog, K3tog, K2tog, put these last 3 sts back on LHN and K3tog; P2, K7
Row 8: K15, O, (K2tog)2
Row 9: K3, O, K2tog, K1, c3, P4, P3so, K3, c3, P4, P3so, K1, (O2, K2tog)3
Row 10: (K2, P1)3, K9, O, (K2tog)2
Row 11: K3, O, K2tog, K3, c3, P4, P3so, K12
Row 12: C6, K11, O, (K2tog)2

The cast-on and cast-off edges of the doily illustrated on page 36 were semi-grafted. Substitute any method you may prefer. Time for each repeat: 12 minutes.

Materials: Silver Gauge Category: 'Fine Yarn'.
Pair of needles, sizes 1.50 mm – 2.00 mm (16s – 14s).

Illustration: Coats Mercer Crochet 20, white.
Pair of 1.50 mm (16s) needles.

This edging pattern is very attractive, and not at all difficult to make. The doily illustrated on page 34 had the border **knitted in** with the stitches of the last round of the centre. The join was sewn, but you can use any method you like to make the connection between cast-on and cast-off edge. If you wish to use my special grafting method, leave out the foundation row; work the last pattern row in contrast yarn, instead.

Wicker Edging Pattern

Use a pair of needles, and, using the first stitch of the next round of the central knitting as a base, cast on 14 sts. The last K2tog on the EVEN rows connects the edging to the doily centre.
Foundation Row: K11, O, {K2tog}2 (last K2tog connects edging to doily).

Row   1: K3, O, K2tog, K1, {O2, K2tog}4
Row   2: {K2, P1}4, K3, O, {K2tog}2
Row   3: K3, O, K2tog, K13
Row   4: K15, O, {K2tog}2
Row   5: K3, O, K2tog, K13
Row   6: C4, K10, O, {K2tog}2

Repeat Rows 1–6 as required, or until all the stitches round the **North Star Doily** have been worked off. Join the cast-on and cast-off edges in any way you like.

ABARIS POINT EDGING

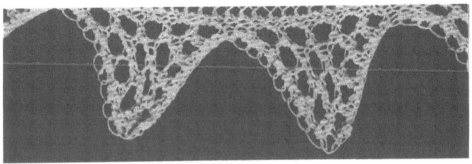

Materials: Silver Gauge Category: 'Very Fine Yarn'.
Pair of needles, sizes 1.00 mm – 1.50 mm (18s – 16s)

Illustration: Coats Mercer Crochet 40, white.
Pair of 1.50 mm (16s) needles.

Abaris Point Pattern (adapted by Tessa Lorant)

Using a pair of needles, cast on 6 stitches in the most appropriate way.
Foundation Row: K*

Row 1: (O, K2tog)2, K1, M, K1		Row 2: O, K2tog, K2, O, K2tog, K1
Row 3: (O, K2tog)2, K1, M, K2		Row 4: O, K2tog, K3, O, K2tog, K1
Row 5: (O, K2tog)2, K1, O2, K2tog, K1		
Row 6: O, K2tog, (K1, O, K2tog)2, K1		
Row 7: (O, K2tog)2, K2, M, K3		Row 8: O, K2tog, K5, O, K2tog, K1
Row 9: (O, K2tog)2, K1, (O2, K2tog)2, K1		
Row 10: O, K2tog, (K1, O, K2tog)3, K1		
Row 11: (O, K2tog)2, K8		Row 12: O, K2togK7, O, K2tog, K1
Row 13: (O, K2tog)2, K1, (O2, K2tog)3, K1		
Row 14: O, K2tog, (K1, O, K2tog)4, K1		
Row 15: (O, K2tog)2, K11		
Row 16: O, K2tog, K10, O, K2tog, K1		
Row 17: (O, K2tog)2, K1, (O2, K2tog)3, O2, K3tog, K1		
Row 18: O, K2tog, (K1, O, K2tog)5, K1		
Row 19: (O, K2tog)2, K14		
Row 20: O, K2tog, K13, O, K2tog, K1		
Row 21: (O, K2tog)2, K1, (O2, K2tog)5, K2tog, pso, K1		
Row 22: O, K2tog, (K1, O, K2tog)6, K1		
Row 23: (O, K2tog)2, K17		
Row 24: C15 (slip first st to be cast off), K2, O, K2tog, K1		

Repeat Rows 1 – 24. Use the **Frill Cast-off** for the C15 if you wish to have a picot edge on both sides of the lace points. Join the edges in any way you like.

SPIDER EDGING

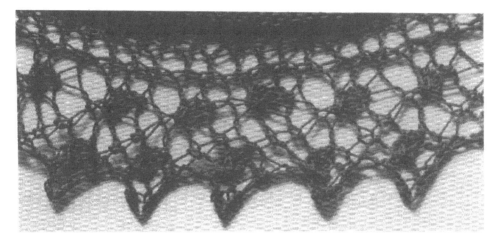

Materials: Silver Gauge Categories: 'Very Fine Yarn; 'Fine Yarn'.
Pair of 1.50 mm - 2.75 mm (16s - 10s) needles.

Illustrations: Coats Mercer Crochet 40; Coats Mercer Crochet 20.
Pair of 1.50 mm (16s) needles; pair of 2.75 mm (12s) needles.

Time: Time taken for one pattern repeat: 4 minutes.

This is another very attractive edging pattern. It is not difficult to make except for the SSK 3tog. The edging works very well in both the finer and heavier yarns. The traditional pattern, shown on page 6, is worked in the heavier yarn and on thicker needles, in an orange colour. It is very effective.

Spider Edging Pattern

Using a pair of needles, cast on 9 stitches.
You can substitute P3tog for K3tog in the pattern, but the effect is not as good.
Knit 1 row plain. Alternatively, prepare for an invisible join (see pages 10 & 11), knitting P7, K2 in contrast yarn. Finish the last row of the last repeat C3 purlwise in the knitting yarn, then work the rest of the row in the contrast yarn. Graft together.

Row   1: (O, K2tog)2, (O, K1)3, O, K2
Row   2: P11, K2
Row   3: (O, K2tog)2, O, K3, O, K1, O, K3, O, K2
Row   4: P15, K2
Row   5: (O, K2tog)2, O, SSK 3tog, O, K1, O, SSK 3tog, O, K2
Row   6: C4 purlwise, P6, K2

Repeat Rows 1 - 6 for the required length.

THE THORN PRESS

WWW.THETHORNPRESS.COM

BOOKS IN PRINT

FICTION

THE DOHLEN INHERITANCE TRILOGY
TESSA LORANT WARBURG
WWW.TESSALORANTWARBURG.COM

THE DOHLEN INHERITANCE
PAPERBACK: ISBN 978-0-906374-06-1
HARDBACK: ISBN 978-0-906374-03-0

HOBGOBLIN GOLD
PAPERBACK: ISBN978-0-906374-08-5

LADYBIRD FLY
PAPERBACK: ISBN 978-0-906374-09-2

A WOMAN'S WORLD, 138-9 CHRI PLUS
HILARY JEROME
WWW.THETHORNPRESS.COM
PAPERBACK: ISBN 978-0-906374-00-9
E-BOOK: ISBN 978-0-906374-36-8

THE MASTER'S TALE, A Titanic Ghost Story
Ann Victoria Roberts
WWW.ANNVICTORIAROBERTS.CO.UK
Paperback: ISBN 978-0-906374-21-4
E-book: ISBN 978-0-906374-39-9

THE GIRL FROM THE LAND OF SMILES
Tessa Lorant Warburg
WWW.TESSALORANTWARBURG.COM
Paperback: ISBN 978-0-906374-30-6
E-book: ISBN 978-0-906374-41-2

SPELLBINDER
Tessa Lorant Warburg
WWW.TESSALORANTWARBURG.COM
Paperback: ISBN 978-0-906374-31-3
E-book: ISBN 978-0-906374-35-1

THOU SHALT NOT KILL
Tessa Lorant Warburg
WWW.TESSALORANTWARBURG.COM
Paperback: ISBN 978-0-906374-28-3
E-book: ISBN 978-0-906374-29-0

CLONER
Emma Lorant
WWW.THETHORNPRESS.COM
PAPERBACK: ISBN 978-0-906374-32-0
E-BOOK: ISBN 978-0-906374-33-7

NON FICTION

SNACK YOURSELF SLIM
Richard Warburg & Tessa Lorant
HTTP://WWW.BUYPATENTIAL.COM
PAPERBACK: ISBN 978-0-906374-05-4
E-BOOK: ISBN 978-0-906374-37-5

LOCAL WRITERS

WORDFALL
The 2010 Anthology from Southampton Writing Buddies
Editor Penny Legg
HTTP://WWW.PENNYLEGG.COM
PAPERBACK: ISBN 978-0-906374-26-9

THORN CONTEMPORARY ARTISTS

BRUSHSTROKES TO SPONGES
RICHARD WARBURG
WWW.BUYPATENTIAL.COM
HARDBACK: ISBN 978-0-906374-43-6
PAPERBACK: ISBN 978-0-906374-40-5
E-BOOK: ISBN 978-0-906374-42-9

SOMERSET SCENES
TEIL
WWW.THETHORNPRESS.COM
HARDBACK: ISBN 978-0-906374-45-0
PAPERBACK: ISBN 978-0-906374-28-3
E-BOOK: ISBN 978-0-906374-34-4

INKTASTIC
ANDREW P JONES
WWW.THETHORNPRESS.COM
PAPERBACK: ISBN 978-0-906374-04-7

Made in the USA
San Bernardino, CA
06 August 2014